The Austrian Business Cycle in the European Context

Forschungsergebnisse der Wirtschaftsuniversität Wien

Band 25

PETER LANG
Frankfurt am Main · Berlin · Bern · Bruxelles · New York · Oxford · Wien

Marcus Scheiblecker

The Austrian Business Cycle in the European Context

PETER LANG
Internationaler Verlag der Wissenschaften

Bibliographic Information published by the Deutsche Nationalbibliothek
The Deutsche Nationalbibliothek lists this publication in the Deutsche Nationalbibliografie; detailed bibliographic data is available in the internet at <http://www.d-nb.de>.

Cover design:
Atelier Platen according to a design of the advertising agency Publique.

University logo of the Vienna University of Economics and Business Administration.
Printed with kindly permission of the University.

Sponsored by the Vienna University of Economics and Business Administration.

ISSN 1613-3056
ISBN 978-3-631-57607-6

www.peterlang.de

Für Lisa und Lucas

Zusammenfassung

Die Datierung konjunktureller Wendepunkte stellt nach wie vor eine wichtige Information für wirtschaftspolitische Entscheidungen dar. Die vorliegende Studie ermittelt den österreichischen Konjunkturverlauf für die Zeit zwischen 1976 und 2005 auf Basis von Daten der vierteljährlichen volkswirtschaftlichen Gesamtrechung Österreichs, Deutschlands und des Euro-Raums. Drei unterschiedliche Filtermethoden kommen für die Extraktion konjunktureller Schwankungen zur Anwendung: Differenzen erster Ordnung, der Hodrick-Prescott-Filter und der Baxter-King-Filter. Basierend auf diesen Ergebnissen wird der Konjunkturverlauf anhand zweier Verfahren ermittelt: der Ad-hoc-Bestimmung der Konjunkturkomponente und der Erstellung eines dynamischen Faktormodells, welches die gemeinsamen zyklischen Schwankungen in Österreich, im Euro-Raum und in Deutschland berücksichtigt. Die Datierung des Konjunkturzyklus erfolgt danach durch den Bry-Boschan-Algorythmus. Die Ergebnisse werden interpretiert und mit bereits bestehenden Studien über Konjunkturschwankungen im Euro-Raum und in Österreich verglichen.

Abstract

The dating of business cycle turning points is still an important basis for economic policy decisions. The present study sets out to trace the Austrian business cycle for the Austrian economy for the period between 1976 und 2005, using quarterly national accounts data of Austria, Germany and the euro area. Three different filtering methods are applied: first-order differences, the Hodrick-Prescott filter and the Baxter-King filter. To all of them, two different methods of determining the business cycle are applied: the ad-hoc identification of the cyclical component and a dynamic factor model, taking into account the common cyclical variations for Austria, the euro area and the German economy. Subsequently, the Bry-Boschan algorithm serves to identify peaks and troughs of the cycle. Finally, the results are interpreted and compared with those of earlier studies on the euro area and the Austrian business cycle.

Table of contents

List of figures and tables

List of abbreviations

AR	auto-regressive
aut	Austria
BC	business cycle
BK filter	Baxter-King filter
CEPR	Center of Economic Research
EABCN	Euro Area Business Cycle Network
ESA95	European System of Accounts 1995
eur	euro area of 12 member states till 2006
fod	first-order differences
FISIM	financial intermediation services indirectly measured
GDP	gross domestic product
ger	Germany
GVA	gross value added
HP filter	Hodrick-Prescott filter
MS-VAR	Markov-switching vector auto-regressive model
NACE	Nomenclature générale des ACtivités Economiques; for specific extensions see chapter 2
NBER	National Bureau of Economic Research

P	peak (of a business cycle)
SARIMA	seasonal auto-regressive integrated moving average model
SNA93	System of Natinal Accounts 1993
T	trough (of a business cycle)
TAR	threshold auto-regressive model
TRAMO-SEATS	"Time series Regression with ARIMA noise, Missing values and Outliers", and "Signal Extraction in ARIMA Time Series" (*Gómez – Maravall*, 1992)
X12-ARIMA	program for seasonal adjustment of the US-Census Bureau

List of variables

Variable names are composed of two parts

The first part depicts the geographical region:

aut	Austria
ger	Germany
eur	euro area

The second part refers to the sectoral aggregate:

F	NACE F: value added of the construction sector
CDE	NACE C+D+E: value added of the industrial sector (including mining and quarrying and electricity)
GHI	NACE G+H+I: value added of services in trade, restaurants, transport and communication
JK	NACE J+K: value added of services in financial intermediation, real estate and business activities
GVA	gross value added of the whole economy
GVAex	gross value added of the whole economy excluding agriculture and forestry
GDP	gross domestic product
GDPex	euro area GDP excluding Germany and Austria

1. Research motivation and overview

The dating of business cycle turning points is still an important basis for economic policy decisions. Turning points mark the point of time at which booms end and recessions are overcome. Hence, they provide important information for initiating and terminating counter-cyclical policy action. Fiscal policy interventions suffer from recognition, legislation and execution time lags and also monetary actions take time to work their way through the economy. In order to reap the benefits of stabilisation policy[1], it is necessary to forecast turning points or at least to identify them timely. For both tasks, investigation into the history of turning points – with an exact dating scheme – is crucial, as it can serve as a benchmark for setting up real time based models.

Regular revisions of the economic data set, changes in methodology for measuring total economic output (like the introduction of the ESA regulation for European countries), the adoption of new statistical methods for price adjustments and further innovations make a regular update of business cycle analysis necessary also for past periods. Furthermore, economic research frequently brings forth new sophisticated methods for business cycle analysis, often supported by enhanced computational possibilities.

Despite the fact that business cycle variations are mostly understood to be a demand-based phenomenon there is merit in studying them also on a sectoral basis. According to the classical definition of the business cycle by *Burns – Mitchell* (1946), business cycles are a type of fluctuation found in aggregate economic activity. This does not necessarily mean that the object of observation has

---

[1] Examples for recent estimations of the costs of business cycle fluctuations are *Reis* (2005) and *Dellas* (2003). *Barlevy* (2004) gives a good overview about methods and empirical results.

to be an indicator of aggregate economic activity like GDP[2]. A comovement of such fluctuations in other economic time series – whether interrelated or not – would also fulfil this criterion.

Long – Plosser (1983) stressed the comovements of sectoral output fluctuations as being one of the important features of business cycles. *Hornstein* (2000) found, that these sectoral links show up in several time series like gross output, value added and materials and energy use. *Rebelo* (2005) supplied evidence for the strong correlation between hours employed by industry and total hours employed by the private sector. This strong comovement in economic time series like sectoral output[3] probably induced *Lucas* (1977) to argue that business cycles were driven by aggregate shocks and not by sector-specific ones.

Despite the widely accepted view of the existence of only one business cycle driven by aggregated shocks, these variations can show up in sectoral time series with different amplitudes and with some lagging or leading characteristics. Indeed, the prominent NBER approach for detecting business cycles is based on sorting the different time series by their leading and lagging properties.

Beside the view that supports the existence of only one business cycle, studies based on band pass filters and spectral analysis methods reveal several cycles, all of which represent frequencies qualifying them for being business cycles. Apart from this, there are also statistical reasons for observing business cycle movements at the detailed sectoral level. It is quite easy to understand that if a

---

2 In fact, most studies on business cycles concentrate on GDP or industrial production as reference series.

3 The European System of National Accounts uses the term "sectors" only for subdividing the economy by the sectors "government", "private households", "enterprises" and the "external sector". Nevertheless, the English literature uses the term sector for different branches which is followed in the underlying study, too. In the terminology of the European System of National Accounts these are described as "kind of activities".

small open economy gets export impulses from different economic areas (e.g. the US and Europe) these can show up in different economic sectors and interfere with domestic, idiosyncratic cycles[4] [5]. Confounding both cycles by aggregating the underlying time series to a higher total (like the GDP) could hamper a proper identification of the business cycle and therefore give rise to misleading conclusions about timing and size of fluctuations, and thereby to suboptimal or even wrong economic policy reactions.

Observing business cycles at the sectoral level has the great advantage that it sheds light on economic transmission mechanisms, whereas for stabilisation policy purposes its benefits are not so clear. This is based on the notion that the business cycle is mainly driven by fluctuations in demand that can be smoothed by interventions targeting certain demand components[6]. Opposite to this, supply side measures are understood to aim at the trend component only. Therefore classical stabilisation policy i.e. fiscal and monetary policy intends to act on output via demand aggregates, but not on the long-run growth (trend) path. This view has somewhat changed today in that economic policy tries to generate demand by directly targeting the long term growth path[7]. Examples for this are investment premia, public spending for education or subsidies for research and development. Looking at sectoral cycles, apart from giving an insight into transmission mecha-

---

[4] An example can be the international business cycle interfering with a political one of the type mentioned by *Nordhaus* (1975).

[5] The idea of the existence of several independent driving forces has been taken up methodologically by the dynamic common component modelling approach, where several common cyclical factors represent the business cycle.

[6] Prominent exceptions to this are Real Business Cycle models, brought forward by *Kydland – Prescott* (1982). *Blanchard – Quah* (1989) criticise this as lumping together supply and demand shocks whereas only the latter refer to what economists usually regard as business cycles. For a good overview about the actual development and the future relevance of the Real Business Cycle theory see *Rebelo* (2005).

[7] For the Austrian case see e.g. *Aiginger* (2005).

nisms, could guide economic policy by suggesting branch-specific measures, although these could be difficult to implement.

The present study intends not only to date the Austrian business cycle, but also to give information about the leading and lagging properties for several economic branches. Furthermore, their interrelation with corresponding sectors for Germany and to the euro area as a whole will be analysed. This may give insight into the transmission mechanisms from the international business cycle to the Austrian economy. In order to check the robustness of results, several procedures for isolating and analysing the business cycle will be applied that have become popular in recent time. Additionally, the results of dating the Austrian business cycle are compared with earlier studies[8]. Several contributions have recently been published which focus on the correlation between business cycles in different countries, but there is a lack of recent studies for Austria[9] due to its small economic weight. Such analysis has been carried out for GDP as a whole[10] or for industrial production only, but not for different Austrian branches[11].

The focus of this study is on detecting business cycle comovements between countries on a branch level and dating the respective turning points. A timely identification of turning points at

---

[8] *Breuss* (1984) and *Hahn – Walterskirchen* (1992) carried out the last thorough investigations of business cycles for Austria. *Brandner – Neusser* (1992) and *Cheung – Westermann* (1999) investigated into the impact of the German business cycle on the Austrian industrial production.

[9] Exceptions are the rather new studies of *Vijselaar – Albers* (2001) and *Artis – Krolzig – Toro* (2004) where only industrial production is used for determining the Austrian business cycle.

[10] According to *Harding – Pagan* (2002), the use of many series in the approach of *Burns – Mitchell* (1946) in order to gain a synthetic indicator of the business cycle only indicates, that ". . . these were surrogates for a single series, GDP, as that was unavailable to them".

[11] *Rünstler* (1994) is an example for a sectoral study of the Austrian economy, but focuses more on the long-run impact of foreign shocks.

the margin is not the aim of this study, however. This would require the use of business survey data with leading properties and either detrending methods based on non-symmetrical filters or series forecasts based on real-time data in order to circumvent the end-point problem of symmetrical filters. Furthermore, variables which can explain shocks to business cycle variations (for instance oil price and exchange rate variations) are not considered explicitly, as they are assumed to affect all countries observed in the same direction[12] or they feed into the business cycle in the end.

Diagram 1 gives an overview over the typical methodological steps to be taken in business cycle analysis. It presents a stylised flow of several procedures. However, this does not mean that these steps have to be followed consecutively, as some methods cover several of them at the same time. Following this sequence, the underlying study is organised accordingly. The first chapter presents the data and the procedures applied to prepare them for this study. The second deals with the various methods for extracting the business cycle frequencies from the underlying data. Related to this, a literature survey of the various methods with an examination of their theoretical properties and empirical problems is provided. As different methods can produce substantially different results, not one single is chosen for this study but three different ones. In the next chapter several approaches for the identification of the business cycle from the transformed data are presented. Again, different methods are applied in order to check the robustness of results. The fourth chapter addresses the problem of dating and analysing the business cycle for Austria. In the following chapter, the findings on dating, together with some stylised facts, are compared with the results from other studies. The last chapter offers the conclusions.

---

[12] This assumption seems to be justified if the economies considered have similar structures, as it is plausible to assume.

Figure 1: Steps of business cycle analysis

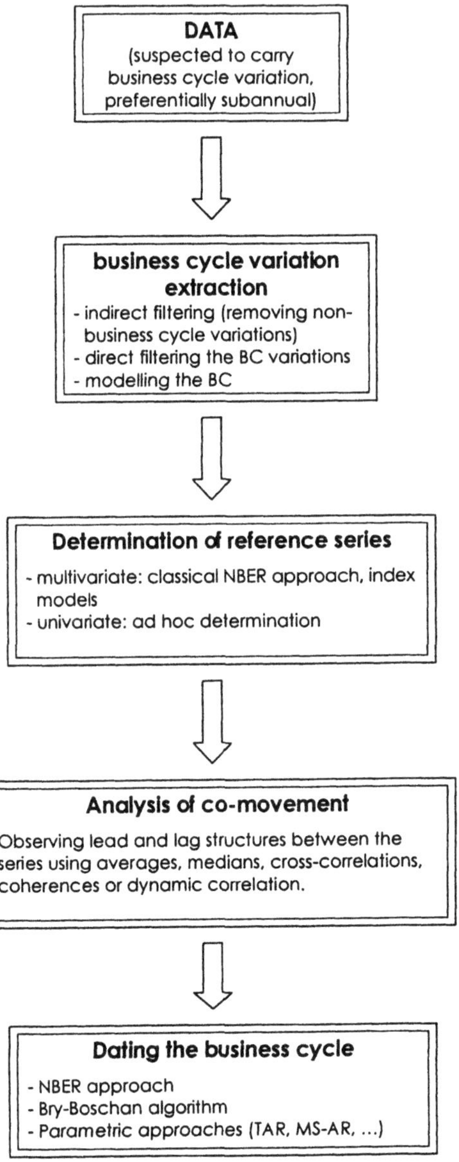

Source: Own illustration.

2. The data

In order to study business cycles on a sectoral basis, only national accounts data broken down by sectors are used here. This is not at odds with the definition of *Burns – Mitchel* (1946) requiring the use of several time series of different origin for business cycle analysis. According to *Harding – Pagan* (2002), this requirement by *Burns – Mitchel* (1946) was due to a historical lack of economic data at frequency lower than a year, rather than a methodological condition.

The following quarterly time series are considered:

- Real[13] GDP as the most comprehensive measure of production. This aggregate has been used in many studies on business cycles.

- Real gross value added (GVA) which is defined as GDP minus taxes on production (like VAT and excise duties) plus subsidies on production (mainly granted for agricultural production)[14]. This aggregate should exhibit stronger cyclical variations than GDP as production taxes and subsidies are empirically not necessarily related to production[15].

- Real gross value added excluding agriculture and forestry (GVAex for short) should show cyclical variations even more clearly than real gross value added and GDP. This is because agriculture and forestry are less driven by business cycle de-

---

[13] In this study, the word "real" refers to chained values with the year 2000 as the reference year.

[14] For time series of older vintage, GVA does not include indirectly measured financial intermediation services (FISIM), which is discussed below.

[15] This does not mean that they develop smoothly. But even if their infra-annual variability is higher than that of GDP, it is to be expected that this lies in part outside the business cycle frequency spectrum.

velopments than by weather conditions. *Boehm* (1998) provides clear empirical evidence for the better suitability of production series adjusted for this primary sector component.

- Real value added of manufacturing at market prices in a wider sense. This includes NACE[16] C (mining and quarrying), NACE D (manufacturing) and NACE E (electricity, gas and water supply). As all these industries include goods producing activities, this is presumably the aggregate showing the largest cyclical variations. For Austria, separate data were available for all three components.

- Real value added at market prices for construction (NACE F).

- The sum of real value added at market prices of wholesale and retail trade (NACE G), hotels and restaurants (NACE H) and transport and communication (NACE I). Despite the relative heterogeneity of these branches, their total is used, as quarterly data are only available at this level of aggregation.

- The sum of real value added at market prices of financial intermediation services (NACE J) and real estate, renting and business activities (NACE K). Again, only their total is available. This aggregate is selected mainly because NACE K contains the production of business-related services, which is supposed to have risen in cyclical variation, recently. This assumption is based on the fact, that industry has outsourced a large number of services in the last decade and increasingly responds to cyclical bottlenecks in productive capacity by resorting to personnel service agencies instead of recruiting own staff. Consequently, it is to be expected that, while industrial output still shows substantial business cycle variations, value added

---

[16] NACE (Nomenclature d'Activités des Communautés Européennes) is the harmonised framework for classifying branches contributing to GDP in EU member states.

should develop somewhat more smoothly and volatility rising in NACE K, instead.

All other economic activities like public administration, social services (containing education and health services) and other community, social and personal services (including culture, sports, etc.) are not considered separately as the production of these services is not assumed to be subject to business cycle variations. Nevertheless, such production is included in GVA and GDP figures.

According to the general view, the typical business cycle lasts from around 2 to 8 years[17]. This calls for the use of economic time series covering some multiples of that time span in order to isolate cyclical frequencies and to identify a representative number of turning points for analytical purposes. Moreover, these series should be consistent so as to measure output over a long period in a similar way. Unfortunately, there have been several events which complicated the search for long and consistent time series, especially for euro area aggregates.

The process of European integration – moving towards a common economic policy in the Union – required a harmonisation of the national accounts framework. Member States have been obliged to compile their GDP data according to the ESA95 regulation. Several further regulations have been passed, focussing particularly on national accounts aggregates. This was necessary because gross national income constitutes the tax base of Member States' contributions to the Union budget. Furthermore, certain development programmes are related to the income of regions or countries and the Stability and Growth Pact is explicitly linked to the development of real GDP.

---

[17] *Burns – Mitchell* (1946) defined it as phases between 6 and 32 quarters, *Harding – Pagan* (2002) between 5 and 32 quarters and there are several studies which take a time span between 8 and 32 quarters as a reference.

The ESA95 itself – being the European version of the United Nations SNA93 – marks a massive change in the interpretation of what has to be recorded as output. Most prominently, computer software was included into output, whereas it was not covered by the definition of production before.

More generally, national accounting is still far from being a static framework of recording production. Recently, all EU Member States had to change over from a fixed base year for price adjustment in national accounts to one of taking the previous year as the base[18]. The re-allocation of indirectly measured financial services (FISIM) was a further big change. These services, provided mainly by banks, are implicitly paid for by the difference in interest rates between loans and deposits. Until recently, they were by convention treated entirely as intermediate consumption by enterprises and therefore not included in GDP. Nowadays, FISIM have to be split up into components of private, government and intermediate consumption, exports and imports.

Revisions – introducing all the statistical innovations referred to – undermined a backward calculation of national accounts data far enough for business cycle analysis. In order to generate longer time series, data sets had to be chained backward.

For **Germany**, consistent seasonally adjusted national accounts time series on a quarterly, as well as on a yearly basis, only go back until 1991. In order to restore data for the period before reunification, seasonally unadjusted data covering only West-Germany but describing a similar sectoral disaggregation have been used for chaining[19]. Thereby, it is implicitly assumed, that the

---

18 The result is a host of time series of two years' length. In order to construct longer time series, growth rates are calculated and chained up using a specific period as reference in order to get long time series in absolute values. Therefore, this method is called "chaining" or "chain-linking".

19 These data have been downloaded form the Federal German Statistical Office website, see www.destatis.de.

cyclical variations for West Germany before 1991 exhibit the same turning points as for the new re-united German economy. Whereas this assumption seems warranted for the turning points, it is probably less so for the amplitudes of these variations. Since planned economies, like the former East Germany, are expected to show smaller cyclical variations, the coefficient of variation for the sum of both areas should be lower than the one produced by chaining. This has to be borne in mind for an appropriate interpretation of business cycle variations. Nevertheless, data have been chained backward as has been done by *Fagan – Henry – Mestre* (2001) for the whole euro area, after a seasonal adjustment procedure.

Due to the German reunification, data for the whole **euro area** also dated back only until 1991. Unlike for Germany, no data – neither annual nor quarterly – were available on a sectoral basis for the euro area. Only a seasonally-adjusted series for total GDP, made available by the Euro Area Business Cycle Network (EABCN)[20] and reaching from to beginning of 1970 till the fourth quarter of 2003, entered the data set. Using the latest euro area GDP data, this series has been extended until the second quarter of 2005.

For **Austria** three data sets have been used to construct quarterly sectoral time series reaching back to the beginning of 1976. The first are annual national accounts data starting 1976, the second quarterly national accounts series reaching back to the first quarter of 1988 which are consistent with the respective annual figures. For chaining back quarterly figures before 1988, national accounts data of an earlier vintage – showing a similar sectoral definition – have been used as a third data set. In order to retain business cycle variations of the annual time series, the process of chaining quarters took account of these annual totals. The method applied

[20] See www.eabcn.org. The method of construction of this series was published by *Fagan – Henry – Mestre* (2001).

is based on the Chow-Lin approach[21], where the earlier quarters were taken as an indicator for distributing annual totals. With this method, sectoral quarterly time series summing up to annual totals have been produced.

The restriction to only sectoral national accounts data does not provide insight into the sources of the business cycle phenomenon, which lies outside this study. Instead, the focus is on transmission mechanisms between sectors i.e. their lead and lag structure, their cyclical variation and their dependence on euro area and German aggregates. Shocks which can potentially explain business cycle variations (like changes in oil prices or exchange rates) are not considered as they are assumed to hit all observed regions or their effect will be transmitted by the cyclical variation from one region to the other over time[22].

---

[21] See *Chow – Lin* (1971).

[22] *Artis – Zhang* (1999) found empirical evidence that there is a connection between exchange rates and the transmission of business cycles across national frontiers.

3. Methods of extracting business cycle characteristics

Before one can study the business cycle, the latter has to be extracted from the underlying time series. For that purpose, at least a vague idea of the nature of the business cycle is necessary.

3.1 Defining the business cycle

From studying the literature it becomes apparent, that there is no consensus about the nature and definition of the business cycle. This lack of a precise definition results first of all from the absence of a widely accepted theory of the business cycle phenomenon. The most prominent approaches relate to demand-side imbalances caused by information asymmetries between economic agents or to supply-side shocks due to technical progress (real business cycle theories). These problems make theory a poor guide for measuring business cycles. Secondly, the empirical approach for discriminating between competing theories is problematic, too. Looking at the behaviour of economic time series, one can see smooth up and down changes (especially if one imagines some kind of simple trend) without any regularities concerning the length or amplitude of a cycle. As a consequence, there exists a plethora of statistical tools and methods for extracting this kind of movements.

3.1.1 The classical business cycle definition

Despite a long tradition in business cycle analysis, starting from the middle of the last century by *Burns – Mitchell* (1946), their definition still forms the basis of one strand of business cycle studies:

"Business cycles are a type of fluctuations found in the aggregate economic activity of nations that organise their work mainly in business enterprises: a cycle consists of expansions occurring at about the same time in many economic activities, followed by similarly general recessions, contractions and revivals which merge into the expansion phase of the next cycle; this sequence of changes is recurrent but not periodic; in duration business cycles vary from more than one year to ten or twelve years; they are not divisible into shorter cycles of similar characters with amplitudes approximating their own."

As such a definition is far too imprecise for being a working base for a study; it has been the subject of several refinements and extensions[23]. This definition, also called the classical definition of the business cycle, has been criticised not only for being imprecise concerning e.g. what constitutes the aggregate economic activity and the pattern of these movements[24], but also for being "measurement without theory"[25]. In order to study the classical business cycle, several economic time series deemed representing the aggregate economic activity are analysed, with trended and stationary time series (e.g. interest rates) both being observed within the same framework. It is not required to separate stationary movements from a trend, only some prior adjustment for working days and seasonal variations is recommended. But, without breaking down changes in economic activity into trend growth and cyclical movements it may be difficult to interpret the cycle, with problematic consequences for economic policy interventions.

Apart from shortcomings in the theoretical definition, this method does not distinguish between different sources of economic growth and has lost some of its popularity[26]. If this definition of

---

[23] Examples for this are *Zarnowitz* (1992), and *Zarnowitz – Moore* (1982).

[24] See *Harding – Pagan* (2003).

[25] See *Koopmans* (1947).

[26] Whereas business cycle analysis with level data lost its scientific importance in the last decades, there are some recent studies by *Harding – Pagan* (2002), *Hess – Iwata* (1997) and *Clements – Krolzig* (2004) giving evidence for a kind of revival of such approaches.

business cycle is applied where the focus lies on developments in the level of time series, economies showing a strong trend growth will experience only few recessions.

3.1.2 The deviation cycle definition

As business cycles seem to be recurrent but not periodic, as *Burns – Mitchell* (1946) pointed out, *Mintz* (1969) suggested separating the trend from time series in order to study them properly. This was quite in line with *Lucas'* (1977) suggestion of defining the business cycle as the deviations of aggregate real output from trend, which puts the definition on a more theoretical basis. The *Solow* (1970) growth model, describing production as following a secular trend – mostly driven by technological progress – with demand-driven imbalances causing temporary departures (the business cycle) from it, serves here as the theoretical framework. This is probably the definition most people have in mind, when they talk about the business cycle.

If the business cycle is defined as departure from a trend it is called the "deviation cycle" or "growth cycle" approach. As the term "growth" usually refers to growth rates or first order differences in logs – which represents a special method for de-trending time series and therefore a kind of deviation cycle approach- the term "deviation cycle" will always be used henceforth[27].

The choice of the appropriate definition of business cycles – classical or deviation cycle – may depend on the specific research topic. If the purpose is to give guidance for business cycle intervention (as deviations from the steady state growth path imply welfare losses) then the deviation cycle is more appropriate. This is based on the fact, that the business cycle defined by the devia-

---

[27] Sometimes "deviation cycles" and "growth cycles" are used as synonyms; in this case, calculating first differences for extracting the trend is labelled the "growth rate cycle" approach in order to distinguish between them.

tion concept shows a lead in time vis-à-vis the one interpreted in the classical way. Furthermore, it has to be kept in mind that applying the classical approach yields fewer and shorter contraction phases than the deviation method as documented in *Harding – Pagan* (2002). This may lead to a substantially different business cycle stabilisation policy. Especially the lead property makes deviation cycle approaches more appropriate for economic policy issues. For all those reasons, the following analysis concentrates exclusively on the deviation cycle approach.

3.2 Isolation of business cycle frequencies

Following *Zarnowitz* (1992), economic time series measuring output may be represented in the following form[28]

$$(1) \qquad Y_t = X_t + C_t + S_t + e_t$$

where X_t represents the trend component, C_t the business cycle variation and S_t other components like seasonal, working day or weather effects. e_t represents an error term capturing all residuals like special events and measurement errors. In earlier approaches, all components have been modelled as being deterministic, whereas modern ones understand all or some of them as stochastic processes[29].

---

[28] Frequently this model is specified in logarithms where the underlying model is multiplicative $Y_t = X_t * C_t * S_t * e_t$.

[29] Examples for this kind of models are structural time series models following the approach of *Harvey* (1989) where the trend is modelled as a stochastic process. Also the method of using just growth rates (out of first order differencing process) which implies random walk behaviour of the trend component can be regarded as a stochastic approach.

Even the assumption of orthogonality of trend and cycle has been relaxed by some studies[30], which is in line with *Zarnowitz'* (1992) consideration that trend and cycle are possibly influencing each other.

As theory specifies neither the trend nor the business cycle precisely, there is a large dissent in business cycle research, how the business cycle can be extracted from the underlying time series. As a consequence, several methods for isolating the cyclical component have been proposed.

Based on the component structure given in *Figure 1*, business cycle extraction methods can be classified mainly by three none mutually exclusive characteristics

- direct or indirect
- univariate or multivariate
- model-based or heuristic (filter) techniques

Direct approaches try to extract directly only cyclical variations (according to a specified definition) out of one or more time series, without prior adjustment of other components like trend, seasonality or noise. This class comprises univariate filter techniques like band-pass filters as well as models assuming a special structure for all components[31]. The latter can be constructed in a multi- or univariate manner.

Indirect approaches by contrast, first try to single out other information not belonging to the business cycle in order to obtain the business cycle as the residual. As the data used here are already cleared for seasonal and working day effects, this is mainly a task of separating a trend from the series, eventually followed by some

---

[30] *Dellas* (2003) estimated a business cycle model where trend and cycle interact in a non-trivial way.

[31] See *Harvey* (1989).

smoothing procedure to get rid of high frequency noise variation. The subtraction of deterministic time trends, first order differencing, the Hodrick-Prescott filter, the Christiano-Fitzgerald filter and some ad-hoc moving averages belong to this class. In most cases, several steps have to be combined in order to single out the business cycle.

Model-based approaches estimate all or some components by assuming some specific structure for them. Further model-based approaches concentrate on time series models. As they do not assume a specific structure, they can also be regarded as filter techniques. This goes for instance for the Beveridge-Nelson decomposition where the economic time series is represented as a time series model which is factorised after identification in order to extract the business cycle.

3.2.1 Outliers

A proper identification of the business cycle requires a consistent data base, adjusted for disturbances caused by outliers. This goes for all approaches, whether they are model- or filter-based, direct or indirect methods. According to the decomposition possibilities outlined above, these outliers are contained in most cases in the error term e_t of (1), together with other high frequency noise.

For an initial cleaning of the underlying time series, three different types of outliers had been considered:

- additive outliers
- level shifts
- transitory components.

Additive outliers appear at one point in time and vanish thereafter without having any lasting effect on the further development of the series. In a graphical representation of a time series they are marking a one-time spike in the plot[32].

Level shifts are innovations which mark a break in the time series, shifting the successive mean by a constant value. They appear as an upward or downward step in the time series.

Transitory components are outliers lasting only for a limited time and vanishing thereafter. They are either fading out in successive time periods (decay) or they evolve slowly over time and vanish suddenly (ramp).

Some of these outliers can be explained by variables outside this model. Ignored working day variables or weather conditions – influencing the economic output – are examples. Furthermore, every unusual strong movement in the history of a time series may appear as an outlier. In this special case here, this goes for sharp recessions, too. It is a difficult task to detect outliers and one has to define first of all what should be considered an outlier and by which value it has to be replaced.

For the present study, outlier detection has been carried out by modelling all time series as seasonal ARIMA models with regression effects (sometimes also called Reg-SARIMA models for short), which took care of the varying number of working days of different countries by regressing on them. Several steps of estimation are carried out in order to check whether an elimination of the significant outliers (in this study dummy variables with a t-value higher then 3.8) improves the following model[33]. A purely me-

---

[32] It has to be borne in mind that in a first-order differenced time series an additive outlier marks a spike with a counter-reaction in the next period. If no counter-reaction follows, it appears as a level shift in the original series.

[33] This procedure was assisted by the software package TRAMO developed by *Gomez – Maravall* (1992). It is widely used also in business cycle studies like for example in *Artis – Krolzig – Toro* (2004), *Artis – Marcellino – Proietti* (2004) and *Altissimo et al.* (2001).

chanical detection procedure according to some statistical criterion can substantially influence the result of a study. In order to avoid these pitfalls, outliers have been discussed with experts and considered in the light of economic history.

3.2.2 *Calendar effects*

Apart from the business cycle, the varying number of working days influences economic output, too. Therefore, time series have to be cleaned for this influence. As far as they have not already been derived from the data base in adjusted form, this adjustment was made by the same SARIMA model combined with a regression on working day information as it was used for seasonal adjustment. As not only the varying number of working days constitutes the calendar effect, but also Easter and the leap year effect[34], their influence had been considered, too.

Apart from testing for a significant Easter and leap year effect, two specifications for modelling the working day effect have been applied. One tests for the significance of the varying number of working days in total and the other checks for all working days separately. Thus, the regression includes the number of Mondays, Tuesdays, and so on. The discrimination between the two specifications was done according to their t-values and auto-correlation properties of the residuals from the SARIMA model estimation.

In most applications, as in this study, calendar effects are cleaned from the series under the assumption that they are independent from other components like the trend or the cycle. This orthogonality assumption can be challenged by considerations of possibly larger working day effects in times of high capacity utilisation. During recessions a large number of employees have to work part time and their productivity is probably quite low, so that an addi-

---

[34] Other holidays like Christmas have not to be considered separately, as they occur always in the same quarter of the year.

tional working day due to specific calendar constellations will not yield the same value added as in a boom. As a consequence, the business cycle reaction of calendar effects shows up wrongly in the business cycle itself, if calendar effects are estimated as being orthogonal. But this should bias only the amplitude of the business cycle, but not interfere with the dating of the cycle.

3.2.3 Seasonal variations

These high frequency movements can interfere with the dating of the overall peaks and troughs. *Sims* (1993) and *Hansen – Sargent* (1993) have shown that seasonal pre-filtering is essential in business cycle analysis in order to avoid a distortion of the business cycle pattern.

Therefore, the largest part of studies is based on the analysis of seasonally adjusted time series, but there are also good arguments for considering unadjusted series as well. *Cubadda* (1999) found that in the case of existence of seasonal co-integration between analysed time series, the results for unadjusted and adjusted time series can be different. Despite the theoretically difficult economic implication of having a steady state trend showing seasonal variations, he argues in favour of using unadjusted time series and clearing them for seasonal variations within the same framework used for business cycle analysis. In a similar direction points the study by *Jäger – Kunst* (1990) who showed that the process of seasonal adjustment spuriously amplifies the persistence of variables.

There are several approaches of clearing for seasonal variations which estimate the trend and the cycle within one framework, as proposed by *Cubadda* (1999)[35]. In unobserved components

---

[35] It has to be noted, that the application of band-pass filters for frequencies of the business cycle not only cancels out the trend component but also seasonal variations. It is unclear whether this is conforming to a separation process within one framework in the sense of *Cubadda* (1999).

models, this is done either by assuming a fixed trigonometric movement of seasonality[36] or by regressing on dummy variables. In both cases, seasonality is modelled as being stable over the whole time span of the series, which seems to be a rather strong assumption. So the advantage of isolating the seasonal variation within the same framework used for identification of the business cycle has to be weighed against the advantage of allowing for a flexible trend for seasonal variations.

The most popular methods for univariate seasonal extraction are X-12 from the US-Census Bureau and TRAMO-SEATS developed by the Bank of Spain[37]. Both procedures allow – in contrast to unobserved component models with a basic structure – a variation of the seasonal component over time. This captures the possibility of moving seasonal patterns due to technical progress or changing economic circumstances[38] which could be very important for cleaning longer time series like the ones used for business cycle analysis.

Weighing the pros and cons of the different approaches, it was decided to separate the seasonal component externally. This was done using the TRAMO-SEATS software. *Fiorentini – Planas* (2003) have shown that business cycle dating is not sensitive to the use of either X-12 or TRAMO-SEATS. This can be seen in *Figure 2*.

Nevertheless, both approaches, the unobserved component model and the univariate time series model, assume orthogonality between seasonal variations and the business cycle, which should be borne in mind when interpreting the respective results.

---

36 *Artis – Marcellino – Proietti* (2004) or *Hahn – Walterskirchen* (1992) are examples for this approach.

37 See *Gomez – Maravall* (1992).

38 Reasons for that could be new processing techniques in the construction sector stabilising output during winter periods or changing seasonal patterns in tourism.

3.2.4 *The trend*

The deviation cycle approach requires a separation of the business cycle fluctuations from the trend component of a series. There is no definition of the properties that such a trend should possibly have. There is consensus only about the residual part of time series after de-trending. Cyclical variations should be second order stationary, show some autocorrelation characteristics and are expected to have a cycle frequency of some years. According to several authors[39], this type of cycle is best mirrored in the capacity utilisation of enterprises, which varies auto-regressively without any trend. Therefore, the analysis of business cycles is in most cases based on figures showing these patterns of changing economic activity.

As there is no consensus concerning the shape of the trend, there exists a plethora of approaches to de-trending. Unfortunately, according to *Canova* (1998), these different methods of de-trending or direct business cycle extraction can give substantially different results for dating the business cycle. Considering this, various methods of de-trending will be used in the present study. The selection of these techniques will be based on their popularity as well as their appropriateness for analysing the Austrian business cycle.

In order to judge on the latter, a theoretical evaluation together with reported empirical features of the different approaches will be presented.

3.2.4.1 Deterministic trend

Due to its simplicity, this approach was historically very popular in business cycle analysis. A linear (or log-linear) trend – in most cases obtained by fitting a regression line – was deducted from the time

---

[39] See e.g. *Tichy* (1994) or *Breuss* (1984).

series. The residual is taken to represent the business cycle (and the remaining components). Instead of a linear trend, other polynomial functions of time are possible. With the study of *Nelson – Plosser* (1982), this approach has lost most of its popularity. For the U.S., they found that a large part of economic time series are allegedly difference stationary, where the trend cannot be removed by linear de-trending.

For this reason, this method is not state-of-the-art and should not be considered as an option further on in the present study.

3.2.4.2 Phase-average trend

This is a heuristic method of determining the trend of non-stationary time series, usually applied in the classical business cycle framework for estimating the amplitudes of business cycle variations of trended time series. Basically, it consists of the following steps[40]: After identifying the turning points in the trended time series, it is split up into segments between two consecutive turning points (called "phases"). For each of these segments the mean is calculated (this is the "phase-average"). In order to obtain the trend for the whole series, these averages are combined with a smoothing three-term moving average. As this method of trend extraction requires an ex-ante determination of the turning points, it is not suitable for this study[41].

3.2.4.3 First-order differencing

Here, de-trending is made by deducting the value at time $t-1$ from t in order to get stationary differences (if they are first-order difference stationary which is in most cases assumed or tested). If

---

[40] A detailed description of the full procedure can be found in *Boschan – Ebanks* (1978).

[41] *Breuss* (1984) has used this approach for isolating the Austrian business cycle.

this method is applied to a series for which the logarithm has been taken, the outcome can be interpreted as growth rates.

Therefore the basic assumptions behind the method of applying first-order differences are that the trend component of the series corresponds to a random walk process without drift, that the cyclical component is stationary and that the two components are uncorrelated[42]. The original time series y_t is assumed to have a unit root, which is entirely due to the trend component of the series[43]. This assumption of a random walk trend gives anything but a smooth profile of the trend component, which is for example the case in the Solow growth model. Every shock to this trend will never decay in impact in the future. Nevertheless, this assumption is still popular in empirical economics since the pioneering work of *Nelson – Plosser* (1982) who found unit roots in 13 out of 14 long-term annual US macro series, including real GDP[44].

In the case of a time series model based on seasonally adjusted data, this behaviour can be represented as

$$(2) \qquad y_t = x_t + c_t + \varepsilon_t$$

y_t is our trended aggregate, c_t the cycle to be extracted and ε_t some white noise process where $\varepsilon_t \sim N(0,\sigma^2_\varepsilon)$. The assumption of a random walk trend implies that $x_t = y_{t-1}$ which, entered into *(2)*, gives

---

[42] See *Canova* (1998).

[43] There are also multivariate forms of this approach. *Cheung – Westermann* (1999) estimated the trend of industrial net production as the co-integration relation between Germany and Austria. Business cycle effects are captured by the residual short- run relationship not included in the error correction term.

[44] Since then, several authors (e.g. *Rudebusch*, 1993 and *Diebold – Senhadji*, 1996) have challenged these findings by showing that the testing procedure has not enough power against economically relevant trend-stationary alternatives.

(3) $y_t = y_{t-1} + c_t + \varepsilon_t$

Simple arithmetics isolates the cycle as

(4) $c_t = y_t - y_{t-1} + \varepsilon_t$

It can be seen, that the cyclical component includes the error term, which makes it very erratic and does not show up in the smoothness one would expect from a pure cyclical variation. Furthermore, forming first-order differences does not correspond to a symmetric filter as it generates only differences to past values. This leads to a phase shift of the cyclical component and therefore yields a dating output different from the case of using symmetric filters.

In order to look at the properties of this first-order difference method at the frequency domain, *Figure* 2 depicts the gain function when filtering data that are already seasonally adjusted. The grey shaded area marks the frequency band of the typical business cycle between $\pi/3$ (which corresponds to cycles of 6 quarters length) and $\pi/16$ (corresponding to a length of 32 quarters). The bold red line reveals that the first-order difference filter indeed cancels out frequencies that are located close to zero and therefore can be regarded as variations of the trend component. But it also wipes out mistakenly some spectral mass of the business cycle frequencies in the shaded area. At $\pi/2$, which corresponds to cycles of 4 quarters) there is no spectral mass at all, as the data have been seasonally adjusted beforehand.

A remarkable property of this filter is that it superimposes all higher frequencies, raising the gain for very high frequencies above 1. This explains the very erratic output of the filter as one can see from looking at growth rate series.

Applying first-order differences to processes which are either trend stationary or show a higher degree of integration biases the outcome for business cycle interpretation. In the first case, this would correspond to over-differencing which biases the cyclicality to the high frequency spectrum, whereas in the second case under-differencing shifts it to the low frequency area[45].

Due to these deficiencies, the first-order difference filter has lost most of his popularity in empirical studies on business cycles. If it is used at all, it is mostly to check for robustness of the output across several methods or to illustrate its deficiencies. Despite these undesired properties which limit the use of this filter for business cycle analysis, it will be considered in this study due to the popularity of growth-rate-based interpretations as a rule-of-thumb method[46].

3.2.4.4 Hodrick-Prescott filter

The use of the business cycle filter proposed by *Hodrick – Prescott* (1980) is very popular among business cycle researchers. It is a flexible tool that is capable of removing non-stationary components that are integrated of order four or less[47]. Effectively, the trend implicitly fitted by the HP filter amounts to a process of curve fitting. It results from constructing a trend as smooth as possible, with penalizing all squared deviations from this trend from the original time series. The precise formula is

$$(5) \qquad \min_{[g_t]_{t-1}^{T}} \sum_{t=1}^{T} [(y_t - g_t)^2 + \lambda [(g_{t+1} - g_t) - (g_t - g_{t-1})]^2] \quad \lambda \geq 0$$

where y_t is the original trended time series and g_t is the trend to be estimated and subtracted. λ is acting as the signal-to-noise ration, being the weight for penalizing all deviations from trend, which has to be fixed by the user. If $\lambda = 0$, there is no difference between the trend and the original series, if λ approaches infinity

---

[45] See e.g. *Ritschl – Uebele* (2006).

[46] Like it is done by the CEPR Business Cycle Dating Committee.

[47] See *Baxter – King* (1995).

the trend component becomes linear. Typically a value of 1600 is chosen for applications using quarterly data[48]. The HP filter extracts a trend which can be stochastic but moves smoothly over time and is uncorrelated with the cyclical component[49]. A further property is its symmetry, so that no phase shift is introduced. In its ideal representation (its infinite sample version), it approximately places zero weight at the zero frequency (the trend) and close to unit weight at high frequency. This last property leads to a non-trended output but which carries high-frequency information like the noise component e_t. *Figure* 2 depicts the gain function of this filter. It wipes out rather clear-cut all frequencies lower than $\pi/16$ (i.e. cycles longer than 32 quarters) and leaves all other frequencies unchanged (again, the loss of spectral mass at $\pi/2$ is due to the preceding seasonal adjustment process).

In order to overcome the disadvantage of residual high frequencies, sometimes a kind of low-term moving average is applied after the HP filter for smoothing the output. *Artis – Marcellino – Proietti* (2004) used a band-pass version of the HP filter. They combined two HP filters – which both are virtual approximations of high-pass filters – in order to get a smoother output, corresponding to the business cycle frequency band.

The trend resulting from the minimisation process of (5) can also be represented as a linear symmetric filter. Like all symmetric filters, the HP filter is – in its ideal presentation – subjected to the endpoint problem, which means that there is a loss of several observations at the beginning and the end of the series. There exists a trade-off relation concerning symmetric filters, i.e. the more observations one is willing to lose, the more exactly the filtering procedure works. In the case of the practically applied HP filter, there is no such obvious end point problem as there is a kind of built-in me-

---

[48] It can be shown that $\lambda = 1600$ corresponds to a cut-off of frequencies lower than 32 quarters. See e.g. *Prescott* (1986) or *Baxter – King* (1995).

[49] See *Canova* (1998).

chanical forecast feature which allows de-trending even at the endpoints[50]. The HP filter calculates the trend component and identifies the cyclical component as the difference between the original series and the trend component[51]. The end-point problem is therefore concentrated on changes in the trend component. This makes the HP filter very attractive for practical purposes, but the end-point problem is solved at the cost of the accuracy of the filter. Especially at the end points, the filter works imprecisely in that it shows a stronger leakage. This means that some frequencies belonging to the trend can pass, whereas fluctuations of cyclical nature (especially those of low frequency order) are filtered out.

Cogley – Nason (1995) and *Canova* (1998) pointed out that despite the HP filter's ability to de-trend difference stationary time series, it distorts the frequency spectrum so that business cycle extraction could be problematic.

3.2.4.5 The Baxter-King filter

Band-pass filters are understood as frequency filters, which give – in their ideal representation – zero weight to the frequency band to be filtered out and unit weight to the rest[52]. *Baxter – King* (1995) proposed such a filter for business cycle filtering, which is an optimal linear approximation to an ideal band-pass filter. They constructed a band-pass filter by starting from a low-pass filter, which allows all frequencies ω (below or equal a certain threshold $\underline{\omega}$) to pass. This requires that all frequencies get a unit weight β if they are above this threshold and zero otherwise:

---

[50] See *Baxter – King* (1995).

[51] See *Kranendonk – Bonenkamp – Verbruggen* (2004).

[52] In a wider sense, high-pass filters, which filter out all frequencies below a certain frequency threshold (e.g. the trend) as well as low-pass filters, which let pass only frequencies below a certain threshold, can be regarded as band-pass filters. But what is meant here are only the filters which capture the band between two thresholds not belonging to extreme ends.

$$(6) \qquad \beta(\omega)=\begin{cases}1 & \text{if } |\omega| \leq \underline{\omega} \\ 0 & \text{if } |\omega| > \underline{\omega}\end{cases}$$

With the help of these frequency weights $\beta(\omega)$ it is possible to derive the time series filter weights $b(h)$ by applying the inverse Fourier transformation to the frequency response function

$$(7) \qquad b_h = \int_{-\pi}^{\pi} \beta(\omega) e^{i\omega h}\, d\omega$$

The time series filter weights $b(h)$ can be used for constructing the ideal low-pass filter in the time domain

$$(8) \qquad b(L) = \sum_{-\infty}^{\infty} b_h\, L^h$$

This ideal low-pass filter is symmetrical (as it goes from $-\infty$ to $+\infty$) and is constructed as an infinite-order moving average. The weights in this moving average are $b_0 = \underline{\omega}/\pi$, and $b_h = sin(h\underline{\omega})/h\pi$ for h = 1, 2, . . .[53]. In practice, an approximation of this ideal filter will be enough, such that a shorter filter can be applied which solves the end point problem at the cost of a leakage.

From this low-pass filter, a band-pass filter can be easily derived from two consecutive low-pass filters, one working at the lower boundary $\underline{\omega}$ and the other at ϖ. The approximation to this ideal band-pass filter with the weighting scheme derived this way is called the Baxter-King filter or BK filter for short. Its weights are given by

$$(9) \qquad \tilde{b}(L) = \frac{\sin L\overline{\varpi} - \sin L\underline{\omega}}{L\pi} - \frac{1}{2K+1} \sum_{L=-K}^{L=K} \frac{\sin L\overline{\varpi} - \sin L\underline{\omega}}{L\pi}$$

[53] For details the reader is referred to *Baxter – King* (1995).

with again $\underline{\omega}$ and ϖ being the lower and upper boundaries and K representing the length of the filter.

Figure 2: Gain function of stationary transformations

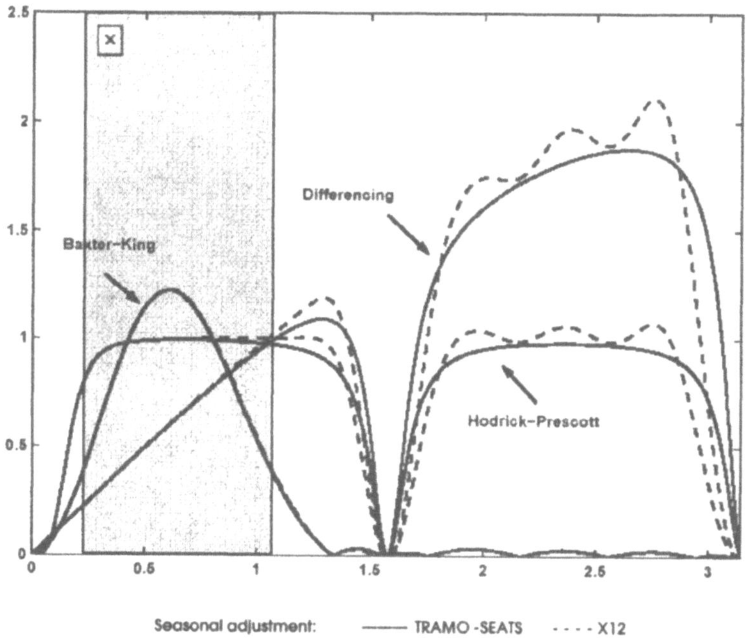

Source: *Fiorentini – Planas* (2003).

The upper and lower boundaries (usually cyclical components between 8 and 32 quarters)[54] are captured, by filtering out all frequencies above or below. Convenient properties of this BK filter are that the identification assumption requires no restriction concerning the trend to be either deterministic or stochastic and it al-

[54] In the frequency domain, this corresponds to a band between $\pi/16$ (= 32 quarters) and $\pi/4$ (= 8 quarters).

lows for changes in the trend behaviour over time as long as the changes are not too frequent[55].

An advantage over the HP filter is that the BK filter cancels out higher frequencies above the cyclical variations, too, whereas the former – acting as a pure high-pass filter – still gives an erratic but de-trended output. This can be seen again in *Figure 2*. The BK filter cancels out lower frequencies dedicated to the trend frequencies below $\pi/3$. This allows the filter to be applied theoretically even to non-seasonally-adjusted series.

A further advantage is that the loss of frequency information due to data aggregation seems to be less of a problem for band-pass filters than for the HP filter. *Aadland* (2005) has shown that aggregated high-pass filtered data (e.g. by the HP filter) can lead to spurious cycles at the business cycle frequencies, if the disaggregated data carried strong variations in the high frequency area. This is due to the so-called "aliasing"-problem which arises when high frequency data are observed at lower frequencies.

As the BK filter is symmetric like the HP filter, it causes no phase shift. A convenient feature of the BK filter is its transparency. The user can explicitly fix the upper and lower level of the band to be filtered; thereby defining what should be understood as the business cycle. Furthermore, the degree of approximation to the ideal band-pass version can be chosen. This can be done by sacrificing observations towards either end point in order to make the filter work more exactly, i.e. to reduce its leakage. The problem of leakage arises with the approximation of the filter. As it is not possible in practice to work with infinitely long time series, shorter filters have to be applied. This has two consequences: First, frequencies can pass which should be filtered out and some are mistakenly filtered out which should pass; and second, frequencies are superimposed at the borders of the frequency band, which appears as

---

[55] See *Canova* (1998).

side-lobes. As *Woitek* (2001) pointed out, this could possibly lead to spurious results in business cycle analysis. But the leakage problem as well as the one of amplified side-lobes can both be reduced by using longer-term filters and sacrificing more observations at either end of the time series.

Applying the BK filter, one has the possibility to individually select the trade-off between the accuracy of the filter and the end-point problem. Compared with this, the HP filter properties depicted in the gain function of *Figure 2* are calculated by accepting a loss of two observations at either end of the time series. It can be seen, that the precision of the filtering process at $\pi/16$ is not as exact as in the BK filter case. Furthermore, the part in the middle of the business cycle frequency band is superimposed (values above 1) and there is some leakage at higher frequencies.

Figure 3 shows how the precision of the filtering process changes if one is willing to sacrifice a higher number of observations at the start and the end of the series. *Figure 3a* shows the gain function obtained by a BK filter with a window length of 6 quarters, causing a loss of 3 quarters at either end. Compared with this, the 12-quarter-window filter (resulting in a loss of 6 quarters at both ends like it is used in our calculations) cuts out more precisely the desired frequencies, without strongly superimposing business cycle frequencies and with a lower leakage. But this precision is obtained at the cost of losing the possibility of analysing the business cycle at the margin. As this is the period for which the dating is most important in order to take timely economic policy measures, this can be regarded as a drawback.

To overcome this problem, some authors propose an extension of the time series by applying forecasting techniques. *Fiorentini – Planas* (2003) propose an ARIMA forecast for that purpose. But all forecasts based on univariate time series methods (without including external information like business survey data) may reduce the end-point problem at the cost of risking forecasting errors of possibly the same size[56].

3.2.4.6 The Christiano-Fitzgerald filter

A somewhat different band-pass filter has been proposed by *Christiano – Fitzgerald* (2003). It also represents an optimal approximation of an ideal band-pass filter, by imposing a somewhat different criterion of optimality. This criterion minimises the sum of the squared approximation errors which are weighted by their spectral density $f_x(\omega)$ of the data being filtered[57].

$$(10) \qquad \min_{\hat{B}_j^{p,f},\, j=-f,\dots,p} \int_{-\pi}^{\pi} \left| B(e^{-i\omega}) - \hat{B}^{p,f}(e^{-i\omega}) \right|^2 f_x(\omega)\, d\omega$$

Furthermore, the filter length is allowed to vary over the time series and is not restricted to being symmetrical. Moving towards the start and the end of the time series the filter becomes more and more asymmetric, which allows circumventing the end-point problem.

Christiano – Fitzgerald (2003) have shown that the length of the BK filter window not only determines the degree of approximation to the ideal band-pass filter, but influences especially its capability of filtering out long-term movements. The filter proposed by them can also be adjusted to filter a specific frequency band, but – in contrast to the BK filter – its length is a result of the optimisation process and cannot be altered by the applier. Therefore, it is not possible to define explicitly the business cycle with regard to a certain frequency band.

---

[56] In order to extend the HP filter, *Kaiser – Maravall* (1999) proposed an IMA (2.2) time series model for forecasting.

[57] The weights are thus generated by a trigonometric function.

Empirical studies of economic time series for the Netherlands carried out by *Kranendonk – Bonenkamp – Verbruggen* (2004) have shown a better performance with regard to revisions of the endpoint output than with the BK filter. Nevertheless, the use of asymmetrical type filters suffers from phase shifts or they contain an implicit forecast (based on past observations), respectively. Whether a thorough forecast combined with the BK filter yields a better performance depends on the specific case.

In the literature, modifications of this approach can be found, like in *Altissimo et al.* (2001) who applied a multivariate Christiano-Fitzgerald filter in order to study business cycles for the euro area. *Goldrian – Lehne* (1999) proposed a further band-pass filter that is not based on a minimisation process, but on the common pattern of weight matrices, instead.

3.2.4.7 The Beveridge-Nelson decomposition

Instead of filtering time series for special frequency bands, *Beveridge – Nelson* (1981) proposed a time series model-based approach. The idea behind is that after fitting a time series model to the underlying data, its structure can be explored in order to separate the trend from the cycle. The fitting of an ARIMA model[58] implicitly models the trend as a stochastic process[59]. The stationary ARMA part is assumed to be (or at least contains) the business cycle.

In order to show some interesting properties of this approach, a simple example is set up. Assuming the underlying time series can be modelled by an ARIMA (0, 1, 1) process, the time series becomes stationary after forming first order differences. This can be

---

[58] In the case of not-seasonally adjusted data, a S-ARIMA model has to be applied.

[59] In most cases it will be of order one, which implicitly yields a random walk process.

represented by a moving average process of order 1 and shows at the same time the cycle:

$$(11) \quad \Delta y_t = e_t + \beta e_{t-1}$$

where Δy_t is the (log) differenced time series, e_t a white noise term and β represents the moving average parameter with $\beta < 1$.

If this expression is solved recursively and the start values are assumed $y_0 = e_0 = 0$, the following expression emerges

$$(12) \quad y_t = \sum_{i=1}^{t} e_i + \beta \sum_{i=1}^{t-1} e_i$$

or

$$(13) \quad y_t = (1+\beta)\sum_{i=1}^{t} e_i - \beta e_t$$

In *(13)* the first term $y_t = (1+\beta)\sum e_i$ is the trend part which – being a random walk process – is the sum of its past shocks, and βe_t represents our stationary cyclical part. Equation *(13)* implies one interesting feature of this kind of splitting the trend from the cycle: The secular as well as the cyclical component are both driven by the same shock at the particular point in time. This means, trend and cycle are perfectly correlated[60]. In order to make this somewhat clearer, we can transform *(13)* to

$$(14) \quad y_t = \left[(1+\beta)\sum_{i=2}^{t} e_{i-1} + (1+\beta) e_t \right] + \beta e_t$$

showing that the trend as well as the cyclical component at time t both depend on shock e. This implication is in stark contrast to the

---

60 See *Canova* (1998), p. 481.

usual assumption of orthogonality of trend and cycle. But it does not necessarily represent a deficiency, as it seems plausible sometimes to see both components influenced by one shock. Admittedly, this means – as criticised by *Blanchard – Quah* (1989) – lumping together supply side shocks, which affect the secular component, and demand-related shocks influencing the cycle.

As the Beveridge-Nelson approach is based on ARIMA time series models, all problems linked to that sort of modelling are carried over to this trend-cycle separation approach. Foremost, applying this kind of modelling the problem is usually not to find a suitable model but to discriminate between the large amounts of feasible ones[61]. The identification of the cycle therefore remains a somewhat arbitrary task and may be challenged in academic discussions. Furthermore, ARIMA models became prominent on account of their good short-run forecasting properties, whereas they perform quite poorly for longer-term projections. As a consequence, one can extract quite different trends and cyclical components from a plethora of suitable models.

3.2.4.8 Unobserved components models

This type of approach intends to model all components explicitly. A special time series structure is modelled for the trend, the cycle, some regression effects like working days, (possibly the season) and even innovations like structural breaks or suspected outliers[62]. This method is thus very flexible and a wide variety of specifications is possible. Usually the trend is modelled as some kind of random walk process, possibly allowing for a drift. A prominent representative of this approach is *Harvey* (1989), who proposed a so-

---

[61] *Christiano – Eichenbaum* (1992) mentioned this problem for practical business cycle analysis.

[62] For instance, *Carvalho – Harvey* (2004) estimated a model for the euro area with a trend evolving stochastically in its slope and level with adding a serially correlated stationary component representing the cycle.

called local linear trend where the level as well as the slope is represented by stochastic processes. Depending on restrictions of the variance of these shocks, deterministic as well as random walks (with or without drift) and smoothly evolving trends can result[63]. This flexibility makes it difficult to judge the appropriateness of unobserved components models for business cycle analysis. In some more simple specifications they come close to the Beveridge-Nelson decomposition method.

Morley – Nelson – Zivot (2002) argue that in the unobserved components framework the common (but not necessary) restriction that trend and cycle are uncorrelated leads to great differences in the cyclical output. Whereas the Beveridge-Nelson decomposition implies that a stochastic trend accounts for most of the variation in output, the cyclical variation is dominant in unobserved components models for their part. Lifting the restriction of trend and cycle being uncorrelated, the two approaches can yield identical decompositions. As *Blanchard – Quah* (1989) assigned supply shocks to the trend and demand shocks to the cycle, the assumption of uncorrelatedness in isolating the cycle can have decisively different consequences for economic policy.

A possible advantage of modelling explicitly all components – as it is done in the unobserved components approach – is that this process can bear closer relation to economic theory than mechanical filtering procedures do. Whereas the purely statistical non-parametric procedures of detrending can be accused of practicing "measurement without theory", *Canova* (1998) accuses all economic-theory-based decompositions as, "at best, attempts to approximate unknown features of a series and therefore subject to specification errors". So, the explicit modelling strategy not only allows capturing theoretical aspects, but also contains several subjective assumptions.

---

[63] *Koopman et al.* (2000) give an overview over how certain combinations of these restrictions affect the trend.

Figure 3a: Gain function of a BK filter with a length of 6 quarters

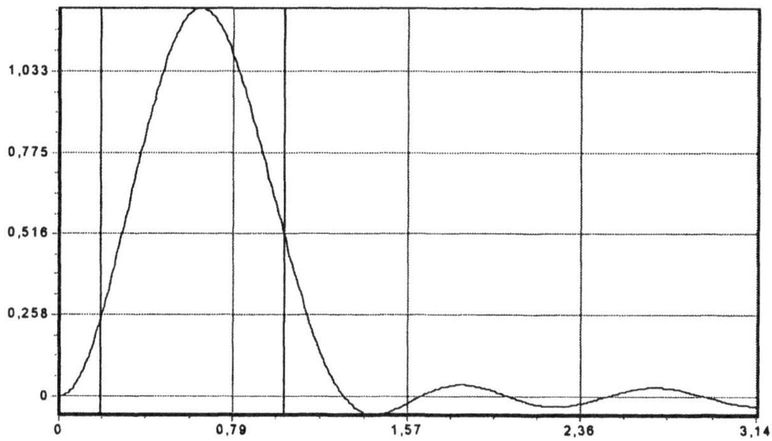

Figure 3b: Gain function of a BK filter with a length of 12 quarters

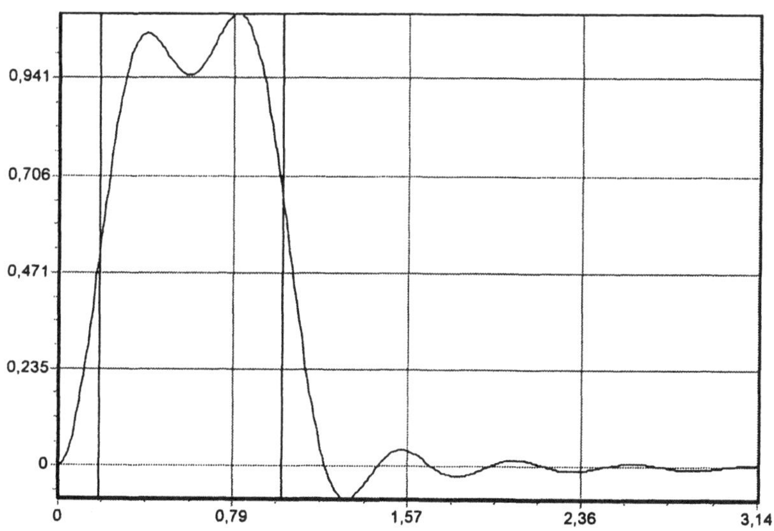

Furthermore, in practical work it sometimes turns out that the results obtained are not substantially different from less sophisticated approaches. For instance, *Hahn – Walterskirchen* (1992) pointed out that if the size of amplitudes is measured by simple variation coefficients of growth rates rather than through calculations by their model, results are largely the same.

4. Identifying the business cycle

After extracting business cycle variations from the underlying time series, either directly by band-pass filters, by explicit modelling in an unobserved components model or indirectly by removing special components, it has to be decided which of the results (or which combination of them) should represent the business cycle. According to *Burns – Mitchell's* (1946) definition, the business cycle is a type of fluctuation found in aggregate economic activity. As they refrained from clarifying what this aggregate economic activity should be, several options are open.

Nowadays, there are ready-made statistics available, which measure some sort of aggregated economic activities. These are weighted by their economic significance in monetary units. Examples are GNI, GDP, gross value added and several aggregates of specific sectors. This variety of aggregates poses the problem to determine which of them is best suited for studying the business cycle. This decision in favour of a certain time series can be made on the basis of theoretical considerations, which is called the ad-hoc method in the present study.

Another possibility is to construct a measure of such an "overall economic activity" out of several economic time series as a kind of index, with a special weighting scheme applied to the time series. Doing this, one has the possibility to include those series which are considered to carry a large content of business cycle information. Furthermore, the weights for their aggregation can be chosen freely. This is of great advantage if series are to be analysed which are not measured in monetary terms, like unemployment rates or interest rates.

4.1 Construction of composite economic indices

4.1.1 The empirical NBER approach

In order to isolate and date the business cycle *Burns – Mitchell* (1946) constructed lagging, leading and coincident composite indices out of a large amount of monthly economic time series[64]. The reason for considering several economic time series was partly the lack of a series covering aggregated output on a sub-annual frequency (like quarterly GDP), and partly the fact that noisy components are reduced through aggregation.

The following illustrates only the basic steps of the empirical NBER approach in order to give an impression of its properties. Good descriptions of the details are provided by *Zarnowitz* (1992) and *Bry – Boschan* (1971), to which the reader is referred.

After a possibly necessary adjustment of all time series for seasonal variations, turning points of them have to be calculated (usually based on the method proposed by *Bry – Boschan* (1971) which will be explained in chapter 6.2). Following this, a reference chronology for determining the leads and lags of each time series based on these turning points has to be set up. This has been done originally by clustering them into groups of leading, lagging and coincident ones on a judgmental basis. Furthermore, synthetic up/down turning point indices (indicating the percentage of time series which show a peak or trough at a certain point in time) or diffusion indices (indicating the percentage of time series in expansion at a certain point in time) are developed. Taking GDP or industrial production as the reference chronology may serve the

---

[64] This method was developed historically at the NBER and still forms the basis of this kind of analysis, carried out by the Conference Board for the US economy or the OECD. Since then, several improvements have been made with every institution having its own special version. The present study only draws on the NBER basic version and the reader is kindly referred to the special literature for variations.

same purpose, but in this case the method comes close to univariate methods like the ones presented in chapter 4.2.

Using this reference chronology, several statistics can be calculated in order to classify the series as leading, lagging or coincident. The most popular statistics in the time domain are cross-correlations and means, medians and standard deviations of leads and lags. In the frequency domain the calculation of coherences is used frequently. Other possible measures – along with their properties – are discussed in chapter 5. As a result, all time series have to be classified into separate sets of leading, lagging and coincident economic time series.

In order to construct one composite index for each class, a specific weight (ranging from 0 to 100) is given to each according to seven properties[65]:

- economic significance
- statistical adequacy (the capability of the series to represent the economic variables)
- timing at recessions an expansions
- conformity with historical business cycles
- smoothness
- timeliness (timely availability of the data)
- stability with regard to revisions

Subsequently, a restriction allowing only the best-performing series (according to these criteria) to enter the composite indices has to be implemented. Again, there are different methods of aggregation in order to obtain only one indicator from several time series. Basically, standardisation methods accounting for the different variabilities of the time series, detrending steps (usually clearing for

---

[65] See *Zarnowitz – Boschan* (1975).

phase-average-trends as presented in 3.2.4.2.) and special heuristic weighting schemes are employed[66].

It is easy to see that the whole process is rather time consuming and hard to track, apart from its high degree of arbitrariness. *Koopmans* (1947) criticised it fiercely for being "measurement without theory". For all these reasons, this method is not considered to be the right one for the present study and will not be pursued hereafter.

4.1.2 Index models

In order to deal with the more or less arbitrary procedure of constructing business cycle indicators in the line of the empirical NBER approach, several more sophisticated multivariate time series approaches have been proposed. The concept behind using index (or factor) models is the estimation of a common driving force (considered to be the business cycle) in a multivariate manner[67]. This multivariate framework for analysing the business cycle can be understood as weighing all time series together in order to identify their common driving force. Weights for aggregating all time series can be determined such as to maximise the variability content of the aggregate in relation to the one of the whole data set.

In the last few years, factor models have become more and more popular in several areas of macro economic analysis. They have been applied for constructing economic indicators[68], in forecast-

---

[66] *Green – Beckman* (1992) give a description of the method employed by the US Bureau of Economic Analysis (BEA) together with some critical remarks.

[67] The idea of extracting common factors for business cycle analysis goes back to *Geweke* (1977) and *Sargent – Sims* (1977).

[68] *Gayer – Genet* (2006) used this approach to derive a weighting scheme for the Joint Harmonized EU Programme of Business and Consumer Survey.

ing, in monetary policy analysis and for business cycle analysis[69]. Their big advantage is that they try to extract common dynamics from a large number of different time series without running out of degrees of freedom. Even if the number of time series observations is lower than the number of variables, this does not constitute a problem. By filtering out common dynamics, the time series are cleaned for idiosyncratic shocks and cycles at the same time. Furthermore, this can be done without making prior assumptions about a special structure of the common or idiosyncratic dynamics. However, the estimation and identification of the number of factors or components is not straightforward and may lead to less than robust results in some cases.

In its simplest form, several time series are to be represented by one common factor and an idiosyncratic part for each of the series. Here p represents the number of time series, each ranging over the time domain 1, . . ., T. The common factor F and an idiosyncratic part u_{it} represent each of the p time series z_i, which can be formalised as

(15) $$z_{i,t} = l_i F_t + u_{i,t} \qquad i = 1,\dots,p$$

l_i is the so-called loading of the factor showing the contribution of the factor to the common driving force F_t represented in time series i. For identification the factor is supposed to be uncorrelated with the idiosyncratic parts u_{it}, and the $u_{i,t-s}$ are also uncorrelated among each other. This single common factor approach can easily be extended to the identification of more than one common factor[70].

---

[69] *Breitung – Eickmeier* (2005) give a rather complete overview of applications of factor models in recent times.

[70] An example for this method is *Peña – Box* (1987).

A drawback of this static approach is that one of the basic features of the business cycle, its auto-regressive development, is not considered since it is assumed that the factors are identically and independently distributed. In order to overcome this drawback, *Stock – Watson* (1989, 1991) proposed a method whereby a single coincident common factor is allowed to move auto-regressively of order 2 and the idiosyncratic ones are represented by AR(1) processes. Again as in *(15)*

(16) $z_{i,t} = \lambda_i F_t + u_{i,t} \qquad i = 1,\dots,p$

but now a special auto-regressive structure is demanded for the factors

(17) $F_t = \phi_1 F_{t-1} + \phi_2 F_{t-2} + \varepsilon_t$

and for the components specific to each time series

(18) $u_{i,t} = \rho u_{i,t-1} + \upsilon_{i,t}$

with ε_t and $\upsilon_{i,t}$ assumed to be white noise terms mutually independent in order to allow a proper identification of the common factors. This is usually done by writing all equations above in state space form (with *(16)* representing the measurement equation and *(17)* and *(18)* the respective transition equations) and generating maximum-likelihood estimators by the Kalman filter.

This approach is capable of extracting a common dynamic factor – showing business cycle AR properties – from the whole set of observed time series. It is also possible to capture more than one common factor, but in this case the identification of the first common factor influences the following. Thus the number of considered common factors is crucial for the output. A further possible drawback of this approach is "that it cannot be directly extended to analyse large data sets due to computational problems", as *Gayer – Genet* (2006) pointed out.

A different method of estimating factor models is the principal component approach. It was originally developed in order to reduce the variance of large data sets by singling out a common component that is capable of representing the largest part of the total variation, by constructing simple linear combinations of it. Each individual time series is represented by one or more common components and some idiosyncratic variation. In the static case, the idiosyncratic parts of all observed time series are either assumed to be mutually uncorrelated (this is called the "strict factor model") or they are allowed to be weakly cross-correlated and heteroskedastic ("approximate factor models")[71]. A proper identification of the common factors with relaxed assumptions – as it is done in the approximate factor model – requires that the number of time series considered exceeds the time dimension by far and theoretically goes to infinity. This allows for the existence of idiosyncratic common movements between business sectors, as long as they are not too dominant. In the latter case they would enter into the common component.

The dynamic version of this type of factor model approach seems to be ideal for business cycle analysis. It allows the common factors to move auto-regressively and the observed time series can be classified as leading, lagging or coincident according to the common component represented by them. Again, some weak cross-correlation between the idiosyncratic components is allowed and the factors are required to be uncorrelated among each other. *Forni et al.* (2000) suggested a generalised dynamic factor model where the dynamic factors are identified in the frequency domain. Instead of observing the cross-correlation matrix in order to identify the dynamic factors, they focus is on the spectral density matrix.

---

[71] In the approximate factor model case, a weak correlation is allowed even between the factors and the idiosyncratic components. See *Breitung – Eickmeier* (2005).

This approach has the advantage that the identified common factors are invariant to their number being identified. The first common factor explains the maximum proportion of total variation of the *p* observed time series, with all further factors showing diminishing explanatory power, till the pth common component completes the total variance of the whole data set. *Forni et al.* (2004) suggest an information criterion for determining the number of factors to be extracted, which concentrates on the amount of common variance that can be explained by the factors.

Again, each time series is represented as the sum of one or more common factors and its residual idiosyncratic component. In the dynamic formulation, the static factors common to all series can be loaded with lead and lag structures, but all are constructed as being mutually orthogonal at all leads and lags. For the idiosyncratic components it can again be assumed that either they are orthogonal to all other idiosyncratic ones (strict factor model) or that some amount of correlation is allowed.

Formally, this problem can be expressed[72]

(19) $\mathbf{z}_t = \gamma_t^q + \zeta_t^q = \mathbf{C}_q\,(L)\,\mathbf{x}_t + \zeta_t^q$

where as $\mathbf{z}_t$ is the $N \times 1$ vector of observed second-order stationary time series at time t. It is represented as the sum of the vector of common components γ_t and the idiosyncratic ζ_t. The common term γ_t itself is constructed by a vector of q orthogonal common components $\mathbf{x}_t$ loaded by time-shifted weights $\mathbf{C}_q\,(L)$, where L stands for the lag operator[73].

---

[72] See *Forni et al.* (2000).

[73] Allowing for a dynamic structure in factor models – which shows up in leading and lagging properties of the loadings – leads to a loss of information at the beginning and the end of the time series. As already mentioned, this endpoint problem is not a disadvantage for the present study, because no real time dating is intended.

Assuming orthogonality between the common and the idiosyncratic parts allows – in the frequency domain – representing the total spectral density matrix $\Sigma(\omega)$ as the sum of the one responsible for the common component and the one of the idiosyncratic part

$$(20) \quad \sum(\omega) = \sum_{\gamma}(\omega) + \sum_{\zeta}(\omega)$$

where ω is a certain frequency within the interval [$-\pi$ and $+\pi$]. This enables the common part γ_t to be identified by analysing the eigen values of the matrix $\Sigma(\omega)$. According to the method proposed by *Forni et al.* (2000), the eigen value solutions of the covariance matrix are ranked by their magnitude, whereby the largest corresponds to the first principal component explaining the largest part of full data variation, the second principal component explains the second largest part of total variation and so on. As the common factor loadings appear with some lead or lag structure, the practical approach for solving this requires a fixing of the number of frequencies at which the spectral density matrix is to be evaluated. *Forni et al.* (2000) recommended the number of frequencies to be observed within the interval [0,2π] as the rounded square root of the time series length divided by four. This should reasonably settle the trade-off between the length of the time series and the quality of the identification output.

The identification of each of the common components is supported by demanding that their variance at several leads and lags inherent in each of the time series is maximised if it is summed up over all time series

$$(21) \quad \max_{t(1 \ldots m)} \sum_{j=1}^{n} \operatorname{var}(\gamma_{j,t}^{q})$$

with n being the number of observed time series and q is again one specific common component. The essential process of identifying one or more common components consists of looking at the eigen values and eigen vectors of the spectral density matrix of the vector containing the original, de-trended data $\mathbf{z}_t$, at certain frequencies[74].

This general dynamic factor model approach has the big advantage that the analysis of leading and lagging features of all time series is not done as usual after determining the business cycle, but that instead it constitutes an essential part of the identification procedure itself.

Unlike the dynamic factor model approach proposed by *Stock – Watson* (1989, 1991), the business cycle is not modelled specifically by demanding some special auto-correlation of some specific order for the factors. This potentially allows common variations that do not belong to the business cycle to be included in the common component, if the data used are not pre-filtered for high frequency movements. An example would be a terrorist attack which influences economic growth for a short period and is possibly felt in a large part of observed time series. Whereas this appears as a common shock – and therefore influences the estimation of the common components – this cannot be regarded as a business cycle phenomenon. The same argument goes for other high-frequency common or idiosyncratic components like seasonal or working day variations.

In the context of the present study, the low number of time series could be a problem for the identification of the common factors. To obtain consistent estimates of the common factors, the number of series should be considerably higher than the number of observations and theoretically go to infinity. This allows idiosyncratic components to be separated from common variations. Recent research by *Boivin – Ng* (2006) shows that under certain circumstances, the number of observed variables can be reduced without losing explanatory power. The authors have shown that in real forecasting exercises 40 time series can yield better results than

---

[74] See *Forni et al.* (2000).

models based on 147 series[75]. This is especially the case if idiosyncratic components are not cross-correlated as it is required in the strict factor model approach. In some cases, adding more time-series (which are probably noisier) lowers the average variation of the common component while assigning more to the idiosyncratic parts[76]. The findings of *Inklaar – Jacobs – Romp* (2003) are a further example that a higher number of series for studying business cycles does not necessarily deliver better results.

In the present study, time series have been carefully selected with regard to their theoretical content concerning business cycle information. Therefore, series belonging to the domain of public services and agriculture and forestry have been discarded from this analysis. For theoretical reasons, they will not facilitate the identification process, but instead bring some noisy information into the data base, hampering a proper identification. Therefore, a reduction of the number of time series will probably improve the outcome. The pre-filtering of time series in order to isolate only business cycle frequencies should improve the identification process of the common component further. Low-order cross correlation of idiosyncratic components is substantially reduced by adjusting for seasonal, working day and irregular variations. The beforementioned facts warrant the expectation that the restriction to somewhat more than 10 time series can still produce meaningful results[77].

---

[75] A further example is *Watson* (2000) who found the gain from going beyond 50 time series being only marginal.

[76] See *Boivin – Ng* (2006).

[77] The chapters that compare our results to ad-hoc methods and other studies confirm this expectation.

4.2 Univariate determination of the business cycle

This encompasses all approaches where one reference series is chosen (eventually after some kind of aggregation process) without recurring to its statistical properties but for its assumed theoretical suitability. *Harding – Pagan* (2002) emphasised that the use of several time series in the NBER approach to represent the business cycle was motivated by a historical lack of aggregated production data (like the quarterly GDP) rather than by methodological considerations. Nowadays, where such time series are widely available, their use seems to be justified as a reference for the business cycle.

First and foremost, GDP – as a compound measure of total production of goods and services – is expected to carry business cycle information. Without denying its suitability, this series includes by definition a lot of components expected to carry no business cycle variations like agriculture or public services. Theoretically, this should not be a problem if one is able to model or filter out precisely only business cycle frequencies. Unfortunately, in practical life the empirical toolbox is far from being that perfect as to distinguish precisely between different shocks and components influencing the time path of a series. Theoretical guidance for the process of selecting the reference series can be of great value.

As described in chapter 2, GDP contains some sectors whose output can reasonably be expected to carry no business cycle information. Agriculture is more dependent on weather conditions than on business conditions. *Boehm* (1998) gives clear empirical evidence for the better suitability of production series adjusted for this primary sector component. We follow this approach in order to avoid the danger that such variations inhibit a proper identification process. Furthermore, taxes on production – like VAT and some excise duties – are at best coincident with regard to the cycle, if not lagging[78], which distorts the exact dating of the business cycle.

In view of such considerations, the gross value added in real terms excluding agriculture (GVAex) was chosen as the reference series, instead of GDP. This means that the business cycle frequencies discovered in this aggregate are assumed to be the most suitable measure of the business cycle for Austria, and dating results for all other series are interpreted in relation to this reference series. A large number of studies use the industrial production index as an ad-hoc basis for measuring the business cycle. Whereas this approach has the major advantage of offering long time series at a monthly frequency, this is not the kind of business cycle *Burns – Mitchell* (1946) had in mind. According to their definition, the business cycle shows up in aggregate economic activity and not only in industrial production.

The univariate ad-hoc determination of the time series which carries most of the business cycle variations is probably the most widely used approach. Studies based on modelling techniques rely heavily on this kind of business cycle determination. There are several studies using multivariate models in business cycle analysis[79], but they are only multivariate in looking at several countries to extract the business cycle by measuring common trends or common cycles directly. But for all of these countries, one type of time series is chosen ad-hoc as being most appropriate for business cycle analysis.

---

[78] National accounts regulations and recommendations require the recording of tax revenues for GDP purposes not on a cash basis, but to adjust them at an accrual basis. If this is done properly, such kind of taxes are at best coincident as a lead seems to be rather implausible for them. In practice however, lagged cash revenues are used which potentially shift included business cycle variations in time.

[79] Examples are the multivariate unobserved component model proposed by *Artis – Marcellino – Proietti* (2004) or *Cheung – Westerman* (1999), who estimated in a multivariate manner the common trend for the industrial production of Austria and Germany.

5. Analysing cyclical comovements

After extracting the business cycle, an analysis about the leading and lagging properties of several economic time series is of great interest[80]. There exists a broad range of statistics in this respect, which can be classified according to their belonging to time or frequency domain statistics. It is worth mentioning that this kind of analysis already forms an implicit part of the dynamic common component approach and constitutes an essential part of the identification and extraction of the business cycle.

5.1 Time domain statistics for analysing comovements

To this class all sort of statistics belong, which exhibit comovements between time series at discrete points in time or for certain intervals. They are mainly based on correlation statistics referring to second moments of time series.

Calculating cross-correlations in order to detect potential leads and lags is the simplest form of identifying comovements between the business cycle and other series. They are constructed as

$$(22) \quad \rho_{b,s}(\tau) = \frac{Cov(z_{b,t}, z_{s,t-\tau})}{\sqrt{Var(z_{b,t})\,Var(z_{s,t})}}$$

with the subscript *b* denoting the business-cycle-carrying time series (i.e. the reference series). $s = 1, \ldots, N$ counts for all other N time series and τ determines the different leads and lags for which cross-correlations are calculated. If $\tau = 0$ the synchronised comovement is observed. The classification as leading or lagging is mainly based on the delay with which the highest cross-correlation is achieved. It can only be regarded as clear-cut, if the cross-

[80] As the dating procedure of the business cycle is so prominent, this will be handled separately in the next chapter together with some analysis on turning points.

correlation is significantly higher than for other leads and lags in close neighbourhood.

5.2 Frequency domain statistics for analysing comovements

Sometimes it is easier to interpret comovements not in the time domain, with discrete time data points, but in the frequency domain. This is especially the case in business cycle analysis where special frequencies or frequency bands are the focus of interest. These statistics can be derived by the Fourier transformation of time domain statistics. So is the cross-spectra the frequency- domain-equivalent of the cross correlation $\rho_{b,i}(\tau)$, like the spectral density function is the equivalent of the auto-correlation function. The cross-spectra of two series for a certain frequency ω is defined as

$$(23)\quad \gamma_{b,s}(\omega) = \frac{1}{2\pi} \sum_{\tau=-\infty}^{\infty} \rho_{b,s}(\tau)\, e^{-i\omega\tau}$$

with ω being a frequency within $[-\pi, \pi]$ and $\rho_{b,s}$ being the cross-correlation as defined in *(22)*. As can be seen in *(23)*, the cross-spectrum contains a complex part which does not cancel out because the cross-correlation function is not symmetric, i.e. $\rho_{b,s}(\tau) \neq \rho_{b,s}(-\tau)$. Therefore, this statistic cannot be interpreted in order to determine leads and lags directly, but has to be transformed into another statistic like the coherence, the phase spectra or the mean delay.

5.2.1 *Coherence*[81]

The coherence measures the linear relatedness of two stationary processes. It can be regarded as the frequency-domain-equivalent to the cross-correlation in the time domain. The output is defined over the interval [0, π] and shows the correlation of the cyclical (or at least stationary) component of the series at each frequency. It is defined by the squared cross-spectrum, divided by the product of the spectral density functions of both series

(24) $$co(\omega) = \frac{\left|\gamma_{b,s}(\omega)\right|^2}{\gamma_{b,b}(\omega)\,\gamma_{s,s}(\omega)}$$

Applying this quadratic transformation ensures that values are real and symmetric. It can be interpreted as the frequency-domain-counterpart to R^2, the well known coefficient of determination, as it shows the proportion of variance of one series explained by the other for a given frequency ω.

But this transformation has a substantial disadvantage. *Croux – Forni – Reichlin* (1999) stressed that this statistic "does not measure correlation at different frequencies, because it disregards the phase difference between variables"[82]. Thus, only the synchronised comovement of two time series, over some specified spectrum or at a certain frequency, can be observed. Whether these frequencies are phase-aligned or not is of no influence to this measure. Related to our problem, the coherence assumes high values if both series show similar frequency gains, irrespective of whether one time series is leading or lagging.

---

[81] In the literature, this measure is sometimes called squared coherence.

[82] See *Croux – Forni – Reichlin* (1999), p. 4.

5.2.2 *Phase spectra and mean delay*

In order to supplement the coherence with a statistic that informs about leading and lagging properties of time series, the phase spectrum can be calculated. This can be done by combining the real and the complex part of the cross-spectrum as defined in (23) and calculating the arcustangens of it in order to obtain the phase angle:

$$(25) \quad \gamma_{b,s}(\omega) = \frac{1}{2\pi} \sum_{\tau=-\infty}^{\infty} \rho_{b,s}(\tau)\, e^{-i\omega\tau} = \left\| \frac{1}{2\pi} \sum_{\tau=-\infty}^{\infty} \rho_{b,s}(\tau) \right\| e^{-iPH(\omega)\tau}$$

where $PH(\omega)$ is the phase-delay-generating function multiplied by a scalar, and further

$$(26) \quad \xi(\omega) = \arctan \frac{1}{2\pi} \sum_{\tau=-\infty}^{\infty} \frac{\rho_{b,s}(\tau)}{PH(\omega)\tau}$$

$\xi(\omega)$ is the phase spectrum over all frequencies, indicating how large the lead (positive numbers) or lag (negative) is. Averaging over a specified frequency band yields the mean delay for this term. In this way one can look at the leading and lagging properties only for frequencies within the business cycle boundaries or for other frequencies in the focus of interest.

5.2.3 *Dynamic correlation*

Another way of overcoming the deficiency of the coherence of not accounting for phase shifts of frequencies has been proposed by *Croux – Forni – Reichlin* (1999). They recommended a measure that looks quite similar to its time-domain-equivalent, the cross-correlation, shown in *(22)*:

$$(27) \quad \tilde{\rho}_{b,s}(\omega) = \frac{\gamma_{b,s}(\omega)}{\sqrt{\gamma_{b,b}(\omega)\gamma_{s,s}(\omega)}}$$

but this time defined only for ω within the interval $[0, \pi)$. This measure is related to coherence – as it shows its real part – but instead of rendering values real by a quadratic transformation, the complex term is cancelled out by summing negative and positive waves of the same frequency. This can be seen in a different representation of

$$(28) \quad \tilde{\rho}_{b,s}(\omega) = \frac{\gamma_{b,s}(\omega) + \gamma_{b,s}(-\omega)}{2}$$

This should not be a drawback as (ω) and $(-\omega)$ have the same periodicity, which is the focus of interest in business cycle analysis. Furthermore, the authors stressed that dynamic correlation observed at a special frequency band is theoretically fully equivalent to static correlation applied to band-pass pre-filtered data accordingly.

5.2.4 Cohesion

In order to analyse the comovement of more than one time series, *Croux – Forni – Reichlin* (1999) proposed a multivariate version of the dynamic correlation index. It is constructed by weighing together all dynamic correlation coefficients as defined in *(27)* and is called cohesion by them

$$(29) \quad coh_b(\omega) = \frac{\sum_{i \neq j} w_i \, w_j \, \tilde{\rho}_{s_i s_j}(\omega)}{\sum_{i \neq j} w_i \, w_j}$$

the ρ_{-s} being again the dynamic correlation coefficients as defined in *(27)* over all combinations of time series except their diagonal elements. The authors suggest choosing the weights according to their economic significance (e.g. by their proportion of contributing to GDP). This statistic has the advantage of allowing to capture common comovements of the underlying set of time series at all frequencies at one glance. This makes it more appropriate for certain tasks than looking at cross-correlations because high values of the latter neither imply nor are implied by co-integration, common cycles or common features[83]. A practical example of application of this statistic can be found in *Croux – Forni – Reichlin* (1999) and in *Partridge – Rickman* (2005).

83 See *Croux – Forni – Reichlin* (1999), p. 1.

6. Dating the business cycle

Only part of the studies on business cycles restricts itself to co-movement analysis. Especially if studies are motivated by cyclical policy intervention (rather than by the identification of structural similarities), the dating of the business cycle is most important. The process of dating can be described as looking for turning points in the business cycle[84]. There is a difference between the definition of turning points in the classical context of business cycle analysis – where the object of study are the absolute levels of some time series – and the interpretation of cyclical deviation. *Figure 4* shows a stylised example of an economic time series – like GDP – consisting of a deterministic trend plus a cyclical variation.

Figure 4: Turning points in the classical and the cyclical deviations approach

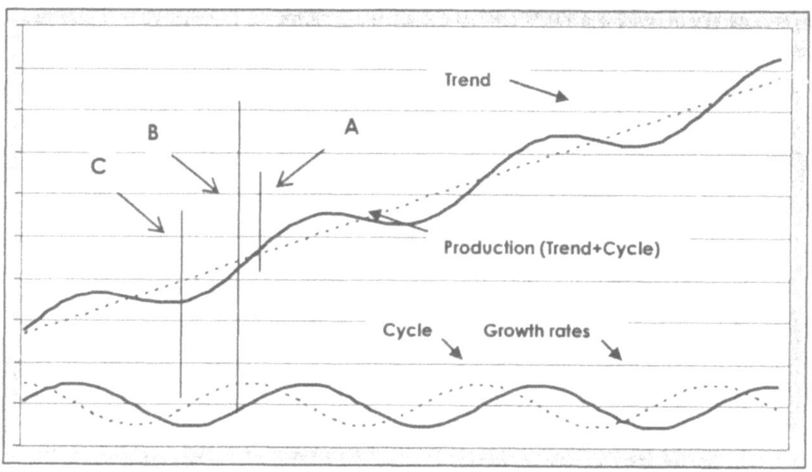

Source: Own illustration.

---

[84] In business cycle analysis turning points are defined in a different way as in geometrics. Whereas the first mark local minima and maxima the latter is the point where a graph starts to change the sign of its curvature.

If the cycle is defined in the classical way, as depicted by the trended bold line in the upper part of *Figure 4*, then point A represents one of the upper turning points occurring at time t_A as it constitutes a local minimum. Following the deviations approach and observing only turning points of the extracted business cycle component, point B marks the upper turning point at time t_B. This point is derived by analysing only the stationary, bold line in the lower part of the figure, which should represent the business cycle according to the deviations approach. It can easily be seen – as it is a well-known fact – that the turning points according to the cyclical deviations approach (bold line in the lower part) lead the ones of the classical definition (bold line in the upper part)[85].

If instead the focus of interest lies on growth rates (growth rate cycle approach), the result is again different turning points. The dotted line in the lower part of *Figure 4* represents the growth rates of the series. When interpreting the business cycle as a sine function (like it is done here with the bold line in the lower part), growth rates follow a cosine function as this is its first derivative. This series of growth rates is illustrated by the dotted line in the lower part of *Figure 4* (for graphical reasons it has been linearly transformed). It reaches its peaks earlier (e.g. at time t_C) than the others[86], which is in part due to its asymmetric construction.

As for their importance, turning points have been given special names. In the classical approach, the lower turning points are called *troughs*, which are followed by a phase of *recovery* leading into a period of *expansion* whose end is marked by the upper turning point, the *peak*. Thereafter, a *contraction* takes place followed

---

[85] The length of the lead is related positively to trend growth and negatively to the amplitude of the series. The higher trend growth, the more it is capable of delaying the downward-sloping effect of the cycle on the whole series.

[86] If a high frequency error term is included, the leading property of growth rates cannot be exploited for an earlier indication of turning points. This is especially true as it has been shown that taking first-order differences superimpose high frequency error terms.

by a *recession* ending with the next *trough*, which completes the cycle. The nomenclature is somewhat different in the deviation cycle approach. The local peaks of the business cycle component – as shown in the lower part of *Figure 4* – are often referred to as *highs* and the lower turning points are called *lows*. Phases between them are called *expansions* or *contractions*.

Having this sequential pattern of the business cycle in mind, dating the turning points has to fulfil several conditions. Firstly, every dating procedure – arbitrary or mechanical – has to ensure that turning points alternate. It must not occur that the turning point following a peak is again a peak. Secondly, the period between the turning points should not be too short in order to allow some economically meaningful process of recovery or contraction. Furthermore, turning points should represent some local minima or maxima according to certain criteria. Several methods have been developed to this end, but only the most important shall be explained here[87].

6.1 The expert approaches

To this class belong all approaches which are mainly based on more or less subjective evaluations, rather than on a mechanical method. The most prominent approach in this area is the dating schedule set up by the NBER. Here, a Business Cycle Dating Committee publishes officially the turning points calendar for the US economy. According to the NBER, a recession is characterised by "a significant decline in economic activity spread across the economy, lasting more than a few months, normally visible in real GDP, real income, employment, industrial production, and wholesale-retail sales[88]." This gives insight into the database that forms

---

[87] Examples for alternative methods not reported here are proposed by *Diebold – Rudebush* (1987), *Wecker* (1979), *Hess – Iwata* (1997) or *Neftci* (1982).

[88] See *The Business Cycle Dating Committee* (2003).

the backbone for the NBER dating procedure. The term "normally visible in real GDP" is not only a hint at the subjectivity of this approach, but has something to do with the availability of GDP, i.e. usually only at a quarterly frequency.

Before this dating can be done, several steps to identify the cycle take place, which have already been described above. Despite its subjectivity, the dates resulting from this approach are not only the official ones, but serve as a benchmark for many innovative new dating methods. This is probably due to the fact, that this approach is adopted by experts who can take into account specific developments in the economy as well as in the underlying time series which could otherwise be misinterpreted if treated in a purely mechanical way. For the same reason, *Breuss* (1984) argues in favour of a re-evaluation of identified turning points by using external knowledge about the characteristics of time series. In case of doubt whether a turning point is dated exactly, an ad-hoc intervention should take place[89].

This was probably the reason why a similar procedure has recently been adopted for the euro area. With the formation of a currency union in 1999, demand for a business cycle dating calendar has emerged with a view to giving adequate guidance to economic policy. To this end, the Centre for Economic Policy Research (CEPR) has set up a committee similar to the one of the NBER for determining the dates of turning points. Its definition of a recession is quite close to that of the NBER, but accommodates for euro area characteristics.

Unlike the NBER, the CEPR focuses on the spread between the EU Member States, whereas the former seems to focus more on sector differences. Furthermore, the CEPR refers to quarterly instead of monthly developments, which has to do with the fact that the

---

[89] The author cites as an example a higher-than-usual economic activity resulting from a front-loading of private expenditure in anticipation of a planned tax rise, which could wrongly be interpreted as an upper turning point.

most reliable economic information for the euro area is only available on a quarterly basis.

Most interestingly, the CEPR concentrates on growth rates. The interpretation of growth rates makes a dating procedure not only sensitive to superimposed error terms (making such dating a poor guide for policy interventions), but also mixes up trend and cycle movements. From a theoretical point of view, it makes a decisive difference whether slow growth results from a gradually sloping trend or a sharp fall in the business cycle.

6.2 The Bry-Boschan routine

The best-known methodical approach is the algorithm proposed by the NBER economists *Bry – Boschan* (1971). This non-parametric method can be applied to seasonally-adjusted trended as well as de-trended monthly time series and tracks quite well turning points for the US as set by the NBER Business Cycle Dating Committee.

This approach starts with a possibly necessary de-trending procedure and the removal of outliers according to some standard deviation criterion. Subsequently, a sequence of smoothing filters is applied, each followed by running the dating procedure. The smoothing process starts with the filter performing the highest degree of smoothness and goes down consecutively till the original (unsmoothed) time series is dated. The final turning points are dated on the basis of the original series, but must be consistent with all earlier dates according to the smoothed series. The specific points are found by checking for local minima and maxima and imposing some criteria for the minimum length of phases and cycles between them. If two or more peaks (or troughs) follow each other, then only the highest (deepest) one enters the dating output.

Disadvantages of the Bry-Boschan routine are that only the alternation of turning point signs and the phase-length impose restrictions for the identification of peaks and troughs. There is no possibility to take into account the amplitude of cyclical variations and, as it is a purely deterministic approach, nor the uncertainty encountered when choosing dates for the turning points.

As this procedure proposed by *Bry – Boschan* (1971) was developed originally only for monthly data, some amendments have been proposed to use it analogically for quarterly series[90]. The version used in this study is the one implemented in the BUSY software package developed by the *Joint Research Centre of the European Commission* (1993). There, de-trended time series are smoothed by a Spencer curve, which is a symmetric 2x7 moving average filter with the following weights

$$\text{(30)} \quad \nu(L) = \frac{1}{320}\begin{bmatrix} 74 + 67(L + L^{-1}) + 46(L^2 + L^{-2}) + 21(L^3 + L^{-3}) + \\ 3(L^4 + L^{-4}) - 5(L^5 + L^{-5}) - 6(L^6 + L^{-6}) - 3(L^7 + L^{-7}) \end{bmatrix}$$

In order to compensate the loss of seven data points on either end of the series, the series is extended by extrapolating the growth of the first and last four observations. This smoothed series is used, first of all, for replacing outliers in the uncorrected series, which are detected by imposing that its standard deviation be a certain multiple of the series total standard deviation, to be defined by the user.

Following this, the series corrected for outliers is filtered by a 2 x 4 term MA term in the quarterly time series case. The output of this filter and the one generated by the Spencer curve are both scanned for common turning points, which are characterised by local minima or maxima with intervals of five periods[91]. Furthermore, a minimum phase length of 6 quarters is imposed, together with an alternation of the signs of the turning points.

---

[90] *Harding – Pagan* (2002) is an example in this respect.

[91] The size of the interval can be altered by the user.

An additional, less smoothed, series is calculated by further shortening to MA order according to a parameter called QCD (quarters of cyclical dominance). This QCD yields the minimum delay for which the average of absolute deviations of growth in the Spencer cycle is larger than that in the irregular component. This series is again checked for common turning points with the series as calculated before, subject to the same requirements for cycle length and the alternation of signs. As this last short filter is able to move close to the end of the series – while for the longer filters synthetic extrapolations had to be made – turning points found in the last or first two observations are dropped.

Versions of the Bry-Boschan routine used for dating the quarterly US-GDP time series have been quite successful in tracking the turning points as published by the NBER[92].

6.3 Hidden Markovian-switching processes

Studies resorting to the method proposed by *Hamilton* (1989) try to represent the business cycle component by a Markov-switching autoregressive model. Here, the series examined is to be represented by a stochastic process that can switch between a contractive and an expansionary regime[93]. In its most general form, not only the mean μ is allowed to vary between both states, but also the AR parameters ϕ of order p and the variance of the error term (with assumed zero mean) e_t.

$$(31) \quad z_t = \mu_{s_t} + \sum_{i=1}^{p} \phi_{s_t} \, z_{t-i} + e_t^{s_t}$$

---

[92] Examples for this kind of studies are *King – Plosser* (1994) and *Harding – Pagan* (2003).

[93] In *Artis – Krolzig – Toro* (2004) a third regime is considered for some countries, in order to capture the effect of a break in trend growth in the second half of the seventies.

with z being the analysed time series and $s_t = 1$ if the economy is in expansion and $s_t = 2$ if it is in contraction, implying that the mean is above or below the average mean of the total series

$$(32) \quad \mu_{s_t} = \begin{cases} \mu_1 > 0 & \text{if } s_t = 1 \\ \mu_2 < 0 & \text{if } s_t = 2 \end{cases}$$

The probability of being in either state of the cycle evolves according to a Markov chain defined by certain transition probabilities for switching from one state to the other

$$(33) \quad \text{prob}\,(s_t = i \mid s_{t-1} = j) = \varepsilon_{i,j} \in (0,1) \quad \forall i, j = 1,2$$

Thus, the probability of being in expansion if the preceding period was also in expansion is $(1-\varepsilon_1)$, or for a contraction following a contraction $(1-\varepsilon_2)$, and the changes from one state to the other are ε_1 or ε_2, respectively.

The estimation of such Markov-switching models is quite complicated, since a global nonlinear process is combined with an unobserved component character. In practice, this is carried out with the Kalman filter technique in order to get Maximum-Likelihood estimators.

As a result, probabilities for each observation of being in either state are obtained, which can be transformed into a binary variable indicating contraction or expansion periods. The advantage of this procedure, compared with the non-parametric approaches, is that for all points in time it can be inferred whether the economy is expanding or contracting[94]. Furthermore, the size of deviation plays a role in the identification process, so that minor ups and downs can be excluded from the dating calendar. The advantage of obtaining probabilities for turning points may be a

---

[94] Except for the very rare points where the probability for either regime is insignificant.

disadvantage at the same time. Usually, there remains a – hopefully small – number of time series points, for which it is inconclusive in which state the economy is. As they are located between expansions and contractions, such points become the focus of interest. If they have to be identified, only a judgemental evaluation can help.

6.4 Threshold autoregressive models

Threshold autoregressive models (TAR) represent a further method of a model-based dating procedure. Here, different regimes (in the case of business cycle analysis there will again be two of them: contraction and expansion) are modelled, with a threshold r for their identification and with a certain threshold delay d to which the threshold refers. The structure is basically the same as in *(31)*

$$(34) \quad z_t = \mu_{s_t} + \sum_{i=1}^{p} \phi_{s_t} z_{t-i} + \varepsilon_t^{s_t}$$

but the process of determining the state is different, in that it depends on a certain threshold (the threshold delay), which has to be exceeded

$$(35) \quad z_{s_t} = \begin{cases} \mu_1 + \sum_{i=1}^{p} \phi_1 z_{t-i} + \varepsilon_t^1 & \text{if } z_{t-d} > r \\ \mu_2 + \sum_{i=1}^{p} \phi_2 z_{t-i} + \varepsilon_t^2 & \text{if } z_{t-d} < r \end{cases}$$

This approach is rather flexible, as for various regimes different auto-correlation behaviours can be modelled as well as separate error term variances. The TAR model is a piecewise linear model which shows non-linear global behaviour. As first steps, the threshold delay d, the threshold r and the order of the AR polynoms for either state have to be estimated. After applying an identification procedure[95] of both processes, the turning points mark the dates of change from one state to the other. As in the case of the Markov-switching model, restrictions for the amplitude of deviations can be formulated and – as it is a probabilistic approach – probabilities for being in a contractive or expansionary state can be generated. However, this can also be seen as problematic, as outlined in the case of the Markov-switching model.

[95] A good presentation of this kind of approach is given by *Tsay* (1989).

7. Analysis of turning points

Following the dating process, an analysis of the turning points gives further insight into the comovement of cycles. This can be done on the basis of the turning points themselves, by comparing their distance from one another or to the ones found in other time series[96]. Furthermore, it is of interest to look at the time series properties at these points in time, in order to get some insight into the strength of the cyclical variation. The following statistics should give greater insight into the duration of cycles and phases, their amplitudes, and whether they behave asymmetrically or co-move with other series. Eventually this can lead to a new dating of the whole business cycle.

7.1 Mean and average leads and lags

When observing the dates of turning points of two different time series (one being regarded as the reference cycle), it is possible to calculate the distance between these turning points. As this distance can vary from cycle to cycle, some summary method is necessary to get an overview of their behaviour over the whole time span. For that purpose, the median conveys a more robust picture of such properties, as some exceptional data points can have a large influence on the mean[97]. Additionally, some thresholds for minimum distances are necessary for the classification of coincident, leading and lagging properties, taking also account of counter-cyclical and unclassifiable relations.

---

[96] A practical application of this method is the construction of the OECD leading indicator. It should give an early signal of business cycle turning points by making use of leading turning points of other economic time series.

[97] It is recommended to use both moments together, as they can deliver important information about the distribution of the lead and lag structures.

The calculation of means of leads and lags can also be done in the frequency domain, looking at the cross-spectrum $\gamma(\omega)$ of both series b and s[98]. As this in general takes on complex values as shown in *(23)*, it has to be transformed into polar coordinates which yield

$$(36) \quad \tilde{\gamma}_{b,s}(\omega) = \left\| \gamma_{b,s}(\omega) \right\| e^{-iPh(\omega)}$$

with the argument $Ph(\omega)$ indicating the shift in the number of periods as a multiple of the frequency for which it is observed (the so called phase angle shift). Averaging over a certain frequency band that lies between the boundaries ω_u and ω_l by

$$(37) \quad \int_{\omega_l}^{\omega_u} \frac{Ph(\omega)}{\omega} d\omega$$

allows looking at leads and lags over this band. Positive values indicate that the observed series z_s is leading the reference series z_b, with negative values indicating lags.

7.2 Contingency tables for turning points

Artis – Krolzig – Toro (2004) proposed a further method of analysing business cycle comovements. With a binary variable indicating whether the economy is expanding or contracting (which can be derived from the turning points) they constructed 2×2 contingency tables for each pair of series of the form of Table 1.

---

98 See *Joint Research Centre of the European Commission* (1993).

Table 1: Contingency table for turning point analysis

Series		Expansion	Contraction	SUBTOTAL
	Expansion	$n_{1,1}$	$n_{1,0}$	$n_{1,x}$
	Contraction	$n_{0,1}$	$n_{0,0}$	$n_{0,x}$
	Subtotal	$n_{x,1}$	$n_{x,0}$	N

Source: Own illustration.

where $n_{1,1}(n_{0,0})$ counts the number of periods when both series are in expansion (contraction) over the whole time span, and $n_{1,0}$ and $n_{0,1}$ how often they are in different phase. By calculating from this some kind of statistic like the Pearson's contingency coefficient one can measure the extent of synchronised comovement of the series.

This Pearson contingency coefficient is defined by

(38) $$Pearson = \sqrt{\frac{\chi^2}{\chi^2 + n}}$$

with

(39) $$\chi^2 = \sum_{i=0}^{1} \sum_{j=0}^{1} \frac{(n_{i,j} - E_{i,j})^2}{E_{i,j}} \quad \text{and} \quad E_{i,j} = \frac{n_{i,x}\, n_{x,j}}{N}$$

The same statistic can be used to determine a leading or lagging property, if one of the time series is shifted by a certain period.

7.3 The intrinsic lead and lag classification of dynamic factor models

In 4.2.1, the index model approach has been presented, with special focus on the dynamic factor model as proposed by *Forni et al.* (2000). This approach tries to capture the dynamics of the whole set of observed time series, by extracting several common components. These components are identified not only by looking at simultaneous comovements, but also by their leading and lagging properties. Such a common component is shown with different intensity in the different time series, as can be observed by the factor loadings necessary to explain the variance of a special series.

In order to make use of the intrinsic lead and lag classification of the dynamic components model, the phase angle shifts of all series compared with (or in relation to) a reference series have to be calculated[99]. This is equivalent to the calculation of mean leads and lags in the frequency domain statistic as presented in 7.1.

7.4 Concordance indicator

A further indicator that offers some insight into the comovement of two series has been proposed by *Harding – Pagan* (2002). They constructed a statistic – called "concordance indicator" – which measures the fraction of time where both series are simultaneously in the same state.

$$
\begin{aligned}
I_{jr} &= n^{-1}\left[\#\{S_{jt}=1, S_{rt}=1\}\right] + n^{-1}\left[\#\{S_{jt}=0, S_{rt}=0\}\right] \\
&= n^{-1}\left\{\sum S_{jt}\,S_{rt} + (1-S_{jt})(1-S_{rt})\right\}
\end{aligned}
\qquad (40)
$$

[99] This reference series can be the common component included in GDP, GVA or industrial production.

where I_{jr} is the concordance indicator between time series j and the reference series r, both of length n, and S_{jt} and S_{rt} being 1 if they are in expansion or 0 if in contraction. It is defined over the interval [1, 0] where 1 indicates total pro-cyclicality and 0 perfect counter-cyclicality. If both are exactly pro-cyclical this concordance indicator is 1 and 0 if they are perfectly counter-cyclical.

This indicator allows no classification of leading and lagging properties of turning points but just of their simultaneous behaviour, if the time series are not shifted in time.

7.5 Standard deviation of the cycle

There are also statistics which concentrate on the size of up- and downturns, as this can be important for economic policy purposes. The simplest statistic in this area is probably the standard deviation of the business cycle component. This measure is constructed as

$$\text{(41)} \quad \sigma = \sqrt{\frac{(\bar{y}_r - y_{rt})^2}{n}}$$

with $\bar{y}_r$ being the mean of the observed series, n the number of observations and y_{rt} the observation itself.

Vijselaar – Albers (2001) used this kind of method to show the exposure of several countries to the euro area cycle. They reported for three different periods the standard deviations of HP-filtered time-series for manufacturing production and GDP. This can be regarded as a simple but crude measure, as it is not clear whether these variations stem from a common or an idiosyncratic cycle, or even from a variation erroneously passing the filter.

7.6 Mean absolute deviation

This measure is constructed similarly to the standard deviation

$$(42) \quad \varsigma = \frac{\sum \left| \bar{y}_r - y_{rt} \right|}{n}$$

Instead of squaring all deviations from the mean (or trend, as in our application) to render them positive for summing up, the mean absolute deviation just cumulates absolute values of these deviations. The use of absolute deviations instead of squared ones should make this statistic more robust in that single large deviations are not weighted by squares. However, *Dickerson – Gibson – Tsakalatos* (1998) found no substantial difference between squared and mean deviations in analysing demand components within the European Union.

7.7 Triangle approximation

Harding – Pagan (2002) proposed a method of estimating the severity/strength of recessions/expansions. They argue that business cycle fluctuations are defined by their deviation from trend as well as by their duration. Therefore, they approximated the area of half of a lobe formed by a business cycle phase by a triangle:

$$(43) \quad C_{Ti} = 0.5\,(D_i \; A_i)$$

with C_{Ti} being the right-angled triangle approximating the area of half a phase of a business cycle representing the cumulative deviations from cyclical neutrality, and D_i and A_i the duration and amplitude of the *i*-th cycle. As the actual cumulative movements (C_i) deviate in practice from the triangle approximation C_{Ti}, a further index measuring excess cumulated movements was proposed by the authors

(44) $E_i = (C_{Ti} - C_i + 0.5\,A_i)/D_i$

in order to remove the bias introduced by approximating the sum of rectangles (which should measure this area) by a triangle. This amended indicator should prove superior in providing some kind of cumulative information about the extent of business cycle fluctuations, as amplitude and duration of the cycle are weighted together. Whether this indicator may give guidance to economic policy makers – as intended by the authors – is questionable, as it assigns equal weights to amplitude and duration. In practice, a severe but short recession probably calls for a different policy reaction than a longer-lasting mild one. Furthermore, in order to serve as a guide for economic policy measures, this information would have to be forecast.

8. Results

In this chapter, several methods of the tool box presented above are applied to various data sets, which are processed with different filtering methods. This combination of methods, data and treatments will give some insight into the robustness of results for dating the Austrian business cycle. Apart from the extensive workload, a comparison of results across all theoretically possible combinations between data sets and methods would be more confusing than enlightening. Therefore, we confine ourselves to the most common or most appropriate combinations, from a theoretical point of view.

8.1 Isolation of business cycle frequencies

As already mentioned in chapter 3, there exist several methods for isolating possible business cycle characteristics from time series. Some of them are indirect in that they try to wipe out all other information that should not be contained in the business cycle component, and others try to isolate the business cycle directly.

It was decided to employ three methods for the present study:

8.1.1 First-order differences

This method was mainly selected for its popularity. Here, first-order differences to the preceding quarter of logged data were constructed, which give approximately growth rates, as it was pointed out in chapter 6.1. Such growth rates are very often used as a rule-of-thumb for dating the business cycle and they are called growth rate cycles.

Using this method for de-trending implicitly assumes that the trend is of stochastic nature and integrated of order 1. As pointed out in the theoretical part, a violation of this *(1)* assumption can shift the true business cycle out of the observed frequency window. It the true order of the process is zero (which means the trend is stationary), building first-order differences would mean an over-differencing of the series, which shifts the spectral mass into the high-frequency area. If, however, the true process is integrated higher than order 1 (which is rather unlikely in the case of economic time series) it is shifted into the low-frequency direction.

This first-order difference filter produces not only rather erratic trend behaviour, but – as can be seen in *(3)* – the cycle includes also an error term. In constructing growth rates this way, the missing-end-of-the-sample problem is solved at the cost of a phase shift and the error variance is superimposed. The latter becomes apparent in the rather erratic movement of this series displayed in Figure 5.

8.1.2 The HP filter

The HP filter solves a lot of problems associated with de-trending reasonably well and is, for its easy application, probably the best practical choice. As it filters out deterministic as well as stochastic trends up to an integration of order four, no strong assumptions concerning the evolution of the trend have to be made implicitly. Due to its symmetry, no phase shift is introduced, and the end-point problem is implicitly solved by a mechanical trend extrapolation. High-frequency noise will remain, but is not superimposed as in the case of first-order differences. For all these reasons, the HP filter is still very popular in the literature and it is applied here, too. For our study, the smoothing parameter λ is set at 1600, as it is most common in applications using quarterly data. According to *Prescott* (1986) and *Baxter – King* (1995) this corresponds to a filter that cancels out frequencies lower than 32 quarters, i.e. 8 years.

8.1.3 The BK filter

From a theoretical point of view, band-pass filters like the one proposed by *Baxter – King* (1995) seem to be most suited for the kind of business cycle studies where the most recent time margin is not in the focus of interest. They directly pay attention to the frequencies which are regarded as the business cycle in the sense of *Burns – Mitchell* (1946). Applying a band-pass filter, a researcher explicitly determines what he or she regards as the business cycle. For the present study, a frequency window ranging from 6 to 32 quarters is regarded as containing the business cycle. All cycles shorter than 1½ years and longer than 8 years are filtered out. Compared with the HP filter, the resulting time series carries less noise (due to the leakage problem discussed earlier, there still remains a small amount of high-frequency variation depending on the size of the filter) and also the problem of extracting spurious cycles – as put forward by *Aaland* (2005) – is reduced. Furthermore, as this filter is symmetric, no phase shift is introduced, but the end-of-sample problem remains. As the aim of this study is not to date the cycle in real time, but to present a robust dating of past cycles, 6 quarters at each end of the series are sacrificed in order to make the filter work very exactly and thereby to reduce the leakage problem.

The band-pass filter proposed by *Cristiano – Fitzgerald* (2003) is not considered in this study. While this filter serves as a good alternative to the Baxter-King filter close to either end of the series, it will hardly offer an improvement within the series, and the weighting scheme is more transparent in the case of the Baxter-King filter. The Beveridge-Nelson decomposition has not been applied, due to its theoretical shortcomings. All shocks influence the trend and the cycle at the same time, which does not seem to be a plausible concept for the largest part of shocks. Furthermore, this method has low power in discriminating between different models; therefore this lack of robustness makes it a poor guide to check the robustness across different methods. Despite the fact that unobserved-components models of a specific structure show some interesting features, they are not considered here either. Again, the large number of possibilities to model the different economic time series components, allow no clear-cut statement about this approach in comparison with others. Results of this method depend more on the capabilities and personal judgements of the modeller than on the method itself. For this reason, only the methods mentioned before are applied to extract business cycle variations[100].

Figure 5: Austrian real GDP filtered

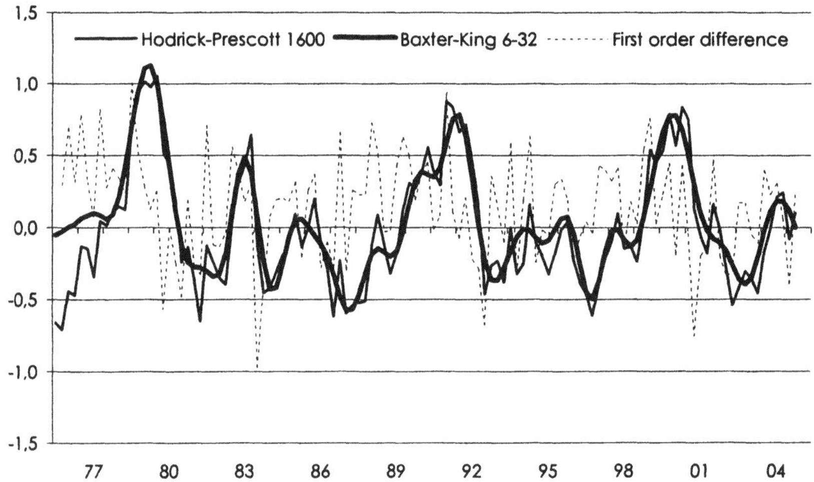

Source: Own calculations.

Figure 5 shows Austria's real GDP at chained 1995 prices, precleaned for seasonal and working day effects and filtered by first-order differences, by the HP filter and by the Baxter-King filter. First-order differences (fod) have been transformed linearly in order to make them graphically comparable with the standardised HP- and BK-filtered series. As expected, the first-order-differenced data show the most erratic picture due to the implied superimposition of high-frequency error terms. Even the time shift of the first-order-differenced data can be seen. It shows some kind of leading property. In 1979, 1981 and 1991, the spike in the first-order-differenced series leads the peaks shown by HP- and BK-filtered

[100] Nevertheless, our results are compared with this kind of models in chapter 9.

data. In 1984 and 1993, this goes also for troughs. While this leading property would be ideal for forecasting business cycle changes, its erratic movement makes this series unsuitable for that task.

If we compare BK- with HP-filtered data, the former appear to evolve more smoothly than the latter which also contain error terms of high variance. But there seems to be no systematic phase shift between the outputs of both methods.

Figure 6: Baxter-King filtered GDP of Austria, Germany and the euro area

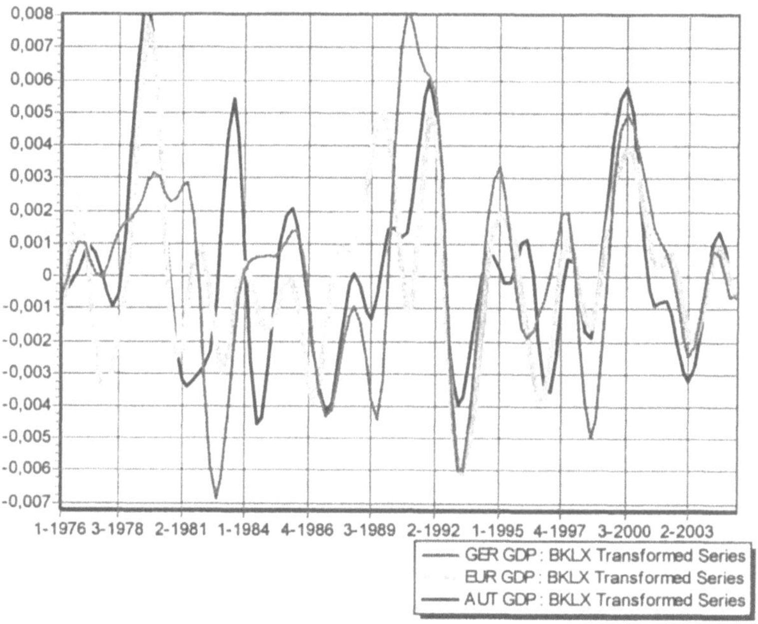

Source: Own calculations.

Figure 6 offers a first insight into possible business cycle comovements between Austria, Germany and the rest of the euro area. Again, real GDP has been filtered by all three methods, but for clarity only BK-filtered data are shown. All series have been centred by their mean and standardised by their variance[101].

Many of the ups and downs of the Austrian GDP (represented by the red line) are mirrored by either the German (blue line) or the euro area component (green line). The number of specific Austrian cycles seems to be limited. A remarkable – nearly countercyclical – movement can be observed in the first half of the eighties, which could also be interpreted as a superimposed leading cycle. In general, no systematic leading or lagging property of the Austrian GDP in relation to the others can be observed; the pattern seems to vary irregularly over time.

As already mentioned, GDP seems to be too crude an indicator for business cycle analysis. Additionally, sectoral cycles have to be observed; therefore, all three types of filters – the first-order-difference filter, the HP filter and the BK filter – have been applied to the following series for Austria and Germany, separately. Again, the time span ranges from 1976 to 2005.

- Manufacturing (NACE C+D+E), including mining and quarrying, electricity, gas and water supply
- Construction (NACE F)
- Wholesale and retail trade (NACE G), hotels and restaurants (NACE H), and transport and communication (NACE I)
- Financial intermediation services (NACE J) and real estate, renting and business activities (NACE K).

---

101 The standardisation by their standard deviations has been done in order to plot them in one figure. With this standardisation, deviations from the mean cannot bee compared between time series.

- Gross value added (GVA) as the sum of all sectors, but excluding agriculture and forestry.
- Real GDP

As described in chapter 2, for the euro area only the GDP series was available, which for the purpose of the dynamic factor model was corrected for German and Austrian GDP, in order to avoid a bias.

8.2 Determination of the reference business cycle

After filtering all time series in order to extract the information content concerning their business cycle variations, the business cycle itself has to be determined. According to *Burns – Mitchell* (1946), the latter is a type of fluctuation found in aggregate economic activity, which would justify the use of GDP as the most comprehensive indicator of aggregate economic activity. But GDP includes also activities which are not influenced by business cycle movements. This is the case for agriculture and forestry, which are more dependent on weather conditions than on overall economic dynamics[102]. Furthermore, it comprises taxes less subsidies on production, which theoretically show at most a lagged comovement with the business cycle[103].

For all these reasons, gross value added of all sectors without agriculture and forestry seems to be closest to the aggregate economic activity in the sense of *Burns – Mitchell* (1946). Therefore, business cycle variations found in that series will represent the ref-

---

[102] Theoretically, higher economic activity can lead to more slaughtering or more tree cuttings as a reaction to rising demand, but according to the national accounts system this represents only a depletion of inventories and not production, the latter being measured by the growth in the number of trees and animals, instead.

[103] This potential lagging property stems from the ESA 95 convention which requires most taxes to be recorded as lagged cash receipts in national accounts.

erence business cycle according to the ad-hoc method. The cyclical components of all other series are analysed in relation to that reference series in order to uncover their leading or lagging properties.

Despite the fact that GVA less agriculture and forestry seems to be a sensible weighted and measured indicator of aggregate economic activity, it does not mean that the driving force behind business cycle fluctuations can best be extracted by analysing that series. A different indicator that weighs together various economic time series of different origin could be more capable of representing the cyclical variations contained in different economic time series. Therefore, a second approach to determine the business cycle has been followed by constructing a composite economic indicator.

As already mentioned in chapter 4, the construction of composite economic indices according to the empirical NBER approach does not seem to be feasible here. As this is basically a rather arbitrary method, an acceptable outcome depends on the contributions by many experts. Instead, a more formal approach is followed in the present study by setting up a dynamic factor model in order to isolate the common driving force of all filtered series.

Thus, two different methods have been chosen to identify the cycle: one ad-hoc method, which determines the business cycle by the cyclical frequencies found in the gross value added excluding agriculture and forestry, and one multivariate approach, based on a composite index which has been constructed by setting up a dynamic factor model.

8.2.1. Ad-hoc selection of the business cycle reference series

In order to get a first idea of the dynamics of the Austrian business cycle, represented by the filtered series of gross value added excluding agriculture and forestry (autGVAex), and a possible comovement with euro area GDP, the following graphs show BK-filtered and the HP-filtered series of both. In order to avoid obstruction, strongly fluctuating first-order differences are not presented.

Despite the included dominant irregular component that has passed the HP filter, some common variability can be seen in *Figure 7*. The development of the filtered Austrian gross value added (again without agriculture and forestry), represented by the red line, seems to follow the green line of the euro area GDP if it departs from the mean. This is strong evidence for a close link existing between both cycles. Only for the early eighties and before, some idiosyncratic extra cycles can be observed for Austria, but since the mid-eighties the comovement seems to have become closer.

Figure 7: HP1600 filtered euro area GDP and Austrian GVAex

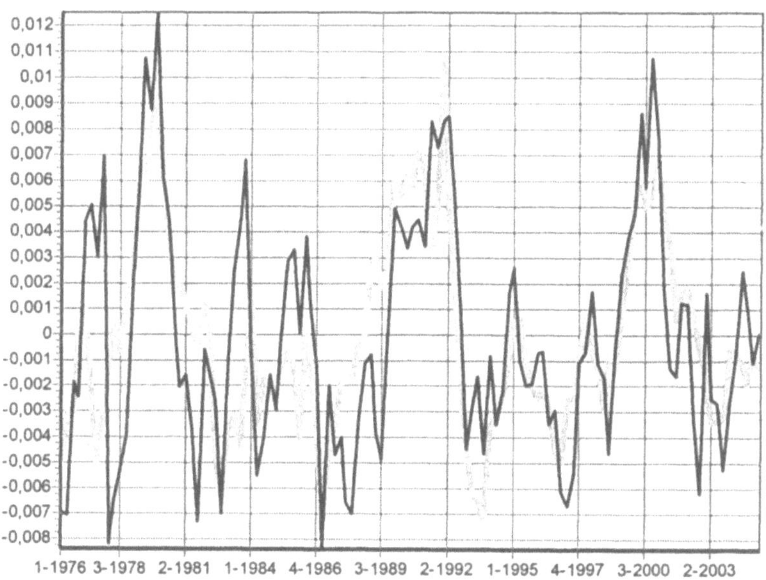

Source: Own calculations.

Figure 8 gives a still clearer picture, as the BK filter cleaned the series for frequencies higher than 6 quarters and lower than 32 quarters[104], with the red line again representing Austria. A strong co-movement of both cycles can again be observed, and the amplitudes seem to have the same relative size. Once more, extra cycles can be observed only at the beginning of the time series. Later on, some synchronisation seems to have taken place. Since the middle of the 1990s, both cycles show a highly synchronised pattern, and the amplitudes seem to have quite the same relative size. This can probably be linked to the accession of Austria to the EU.

Figure 8: BK filtered euro area GDP and Austrian GVAex

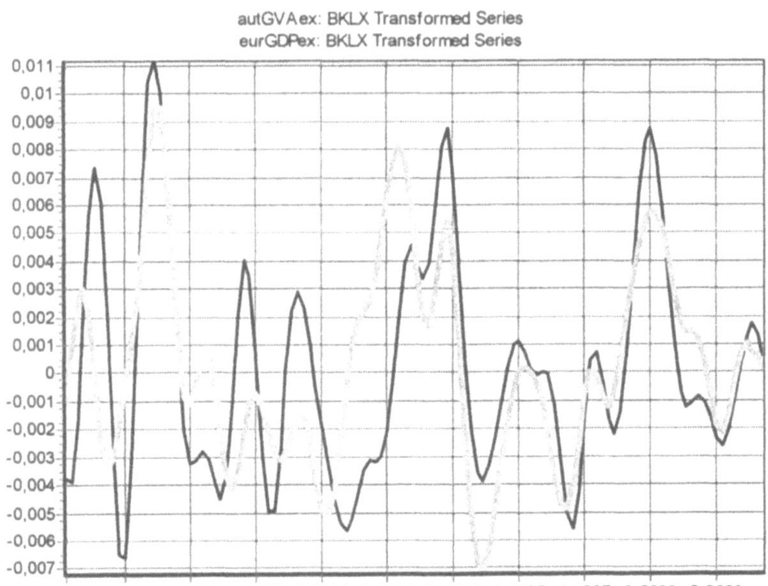

Source: Own calculations.

[104] In the literature, it is most common to set the lower boundary for business cycle frequencies either at eight or six quarters. Here, six quarters have been chosen to take account of the observation that cycles in recent times seem to be rather short.

Less clear-cut is, from visual inspection, the leading property of one of the series compared with the other. Concerning the length of the phases – i.e. the time span between peaks and following troughs – again visual inspection can not reveal any differences.

In order to evaluate the leading or lagging properties of all other filtered time series with respect to the Austrian business cycle, some descriptive statistics have been calculated. *Tables A1 a* to *c* in the annex show the cross-correlations, the coherences, the average spectra and the mean delay for all observed time series in relation to the reference series according to all three methods of cycle extraction. Cross-correlations are calculated as given by (22) in chapter 5. For four leads and lags, correlations have been calculated for the filtered time series with r_{max} showing the maximum cross-correlation.

8.2.1.1 Robustness of cross-correlation statistics

r_0 shows the cross-correlation between a specific series and the reference series at zero lag, i.e. the coincident cross-correlation. The values can range from 1 (perfect cross-correlation at a specific lead or lag) to 0. By construction, they are symmetric and only defined for positive values. The column labelled t_{max} shows the lead (positive figures) or lag (negative figures) at which the highest cross-correlation has been observed. In most cases t_{max} is observed at lag zero, which indicates that this series is coincident with the reference series[105].

Not surprisingly, for all three filtering methods cross-correlations are higher the closer the definition of the series comes to the reference series. Gross value added (this time including agriculture and

---

[105] The reader is reminded of the fact that *Croux – Forni – Reichlin* (1999) had proven that simple static cross-correlation of band-pass filtered data is the same as dynamic correlation over the same frequency band. For this reason, dynamic correlation is not presented in the following.

forestry), for instance, exceeds 0.95 for all methods, being lowest with first-order differences (0.95) and highest with BK-filtered data (0.99). Also GDP, which is very similarly defined as the reference series, shows a high coincident correlation, again with the lowest value of 0.77 in the first-order- difference case and the highest with BK-filtered data (0.87). Gross value added as well as GDP show a coincident cyclical pattern in all cases (indicated by t_{max} = 0), which leads to the conclusion that the two series either exhibit the same cyclical pattern, or that the difference in definitions is not big enough to shift cross-correlations.

Considering the results for the first-order differences and the HP filter, the largest part of the series is coincident with the Austrian reference series. This also holds for the production aggregates, euro area GDP, whether including Germany and Austria (eurGDP) or not (eurGDPex), and for German GDP and gross value added (with or without agriculture and net taxes on production). Only gerGHI, the German service sector covering trade, hotels, transport and telecommunication, and gerJK comprising German financial intermediation services and real estate, renting and business activities are lagging the Austrian cycle. But it should be noted that these cross-correlations are quite low and therefore their lagging property should not be over-emphasised.

Whereas the results of the HP and the first-order difference filter are quite similar, the BK filter gives a different picture. While euro area GDP including Austria and Germany is coincident with the Austrian cycle, the series excluding both countries shows a lead of one quarter. Obviously, the large weight of the German and Austrian economies taken together seems to bias the result in the direction of a comovement. Therefore, the focus should be only on the euro area GDP without both countries. Looking at the cross-correlation of this series, it is highest at a lead of one quarter ($t_{max} = 1$) but the coincident cross-correlation is at 0.63, which is only marginally lower than the one with a one-quarter lead of 0.65. Thus, over the whole time span, it cannot be firmly decided whether the euro area cycle leads the Austrian cycle or coincides with it.

Furthermore, both definitions of German gross value added are again found to be coincident, but GDP shows a lag of one period. This result is in line with theory, since net taxes on production should lag the cycle, although this should again not be over-emphasised because there is hardly any difference between the highest cross-correlation t_{max} and the coincident one. In comparison with the HP- and first-order-difference-filtered data, the Austrian financial intermediation services and real estate, renting and business activities (autJK) are found to have some lag, but again the difference between the maximum and the coincident cross-correlation is quite small, which goes for the German construction industry (gerF), too.

In accordance with the HP and first-order-difference method, gerGHI and gerJK show a lag, which is one period less for the first series. Therefore, the results concerning the lead and lag structure of the observed time series seem to be quite similar between all methods, especially between the ones containing the irregular component, i.e. the HP and the first-order-difference filter. The BK filter shows that the picture is not as clear-cut as the other filters suggest. This might be a hint that part of the cross-correlation between the time series should not be attributed to the business cycle but to higher-frequency dynamics, like special events or weather effects. Defining the business cycle by a narrower frequency band, e.g. only cycles above 8 quarters, will probably show a more pronounced difference between the BK filter and the others.

A check for robustness can be made not only for the leading and lagging properties of the time series, but also for the size of the cross-correlations. The higher the cross-correlation, the stronger is the cyclical comovement between them. This property is important for economic policy decisions, as it signals whether such decisions influence other sectors. *Table 2* shows for each series the differences between the maximum cross-correlations (r_{max}) – for all methods.

The sum over all differences in cross-correlations, given in the last row, shows that the overall difference between the BK and the HP method is rather small, whereas it is substantial compared with the first-order-difference case, especially with the BK method. This finding contrasts with the results for the leading and lagging properties found similar between the first-order differences and the HP method. The superimposition of higher-frequency movements, as it results from the first-order-difference procedure, seems to reduce cross-correlations dramatically. Only for autF (the Austrian construction sector) and autJK (financial intermediation services and real estate, renting and business activities), the cross-correlations calculated on the basis of first-order-difference-filtered data are higher than those of the other methods. It is quite plausible that for the construction sector the methods that include (or superimpose) higher frequency variations (like weather conditions) show a stronger cross-correlation with the reference series (which also includes these variations) than others. But it has to be borne in mind, that this comovement is not one of a business cycle nature and therefore beyond our scope of interest.

As a result, looking only at the highest cross-correlations for different lags, the methods including higher-frequency variations (like the HP filter or the first-order differences) give very similar results. BK-filtered data show a slightly different pattern, but the output shows highest cross-correlations that are not farer away than ±1 quarter compared with the other two methods. Focusing on the size of the highest cross-correlations, largest values can be found in the BK-filter case, followed by the HP-filter output, and the one based on first-order differences are smallest. Only for those sectors where systematic high-frequency variances (like weather or discrete events) could play a role, the methods including this information should show higher cross-correlations.

Table 2: Differences in cross-correlations[1]

	BK minus HP	HP minus fod	BK minus fod
aufF	–0.01	–0.06	–0.07
autCDE	0.06	0.21	0.27
autGDP	0.01	0.09	0.10
autGHI	0.01	0.13	0.14
autGVA	0.01	0.03	0.04
autJK	–0.03	–0.05	–0.08
eurGDP	0.06	0.26	0.32
eurGDPex	0.08	0.21	0.29
gerCDE	0.03	0.26	0.29
gerF	0.09	0.17	0.26
gerGDP	0.07	0.35	0.42
gerGHI	0.07	0.30	0.37
gerGVA	0.07	0.34	0.41
gerGVAex	0.07	0.33	0.40
gerJK	0.01	0.28	0.29
Sum	0.60	2.85	3.45

Source: Own calculations. – [1] For abbreviations used see the list of abbreviations on page B.

8.2.1.2 Coherence

A statistic closely related to the cross-correlation is the coherence, given in the next column of *Tables A 1 a to c*[106]. Instead of showing the linear comovement in the time series domain, it is defined in the frequency domain using cross-spectra, as explained in chapter 5, equation *(23)*. The table shows the proportion of spectral mass within the frequency band between 6 and 32 quarters after smoothing the frequencies by a Bartlett spectral window of three quarters' length. This gives triangular weights $w(n)$ for the frequencies which are calculated according to

---

[106] As the cross-spectrum is also defined over complex values, only the modulus of the squared cross-spectra is taken instead. The root of the resulting squared coherence is used here.

$$(45) \quad w(n) = \frac{2}{N-1}\left(\frac{N-1}{2} - \left|n - \frac{N-1}{2}\right|\right)$$

with N being the length of the filter (e.g. in quarters) and n being an integer number with values $0 \leq n \leq N-1$ which is augmented successively.

The values are ranging from numbers close to 1, indicating a strong comovement within the observed frequency range, to 0 in the case of no comovement. It is clear that time series which are closely defined to the reference series (Austrian GDP or GVA) show a higher coherence than others. It is therefore more informative to concentrate on the others.

Compared across all three filtering methods, the Austrian manufacturing sector shows the largest coherence values, as expected on theoretical grounds. In the first-order-difference case, around 50 percent of the variability observed between 6 and 32 quarters can be explained by co-moving variability. For HP- and BK-filtered data, this amount rises to approximately 75 percent. Such high linear comovement is somewhat biased by the fact that this sector is part of the reference series (autGVAex), but it is also consistent with theory which suggests that manufacturing is strongly subject to business cycle variations[107].

Considering the rest of the Austrian sectors, the construction industry's comovement at the business cycle frequencies with autGVAex is relatively high in the first-order-difference case, at 0.32. The results of the HP- and BK-filtered data do not confirm this, with a value of 0.21 in both cases. Again, weather effects could play a substantial role. The Austrian sector with the lowest coherence is the sector of financial intermediation services and real es-

---

107 Indeed, many studies use manufacturing output or industrial production as ad-hoc reference series for their business cycle analysis. Examples are *Artis – Krolzig – Toro* (2004), *Vijselaar – Albers* (2001) or *Brandner – Neusser* (1992).

tate, renting and business activities (NACE J+K). This result is quite similar to the one in the time series domain. This is not surprising, as the coherence is based on a Fourier transformation of the cross-correlation function and therefore its frequency domain equivalent.

Once again we find that total euro area GDP shows a stronger comovement with the Austrian business cycle than the series corrected for Germany and Austria. All three filtering methods are capturing this bias effect. The German series most closely connected to the Austrian reference series are gross value added with and without agriculture and the manufacturing sector (gerCDE). This result, which is quite in line with theory is robust across all methods and is mirrored in the time domain cross-correlation results. Interestingly, all three methods show that the comovement between the Austrian reference series and Germany's highest-scoring series is not higher than between Austria and the euro area aggregate (corrected for Austria and Germany). This provides strong evidence for the existence of a European business cycle, which would be of great importance for a common economic policy.

8.2.1.3 The mean delay

In order to examine the leading or lagging properties of several time series in the frequency domain, the mean delay – as defined in 5.2.2. – has been calculated and the results are given in *Tables A 1 a to c*. In *Table A 1 a*, the first-order-difference case, none of the time series seem to lead or lag the reference series by more than one quarter. Only autJK – the Austrian sector covering financial services and real estate, renting and business activities – and gerGHI – the German trade, restaurant, transport and communication sector – seem to have a lag close to one quarter (–0.78 or –0.74, respectively).

Whereas cross-correlations and their frequency domain equivalent, the coherences, show a rather similar picture concerning their coincident comovements, the different statistics informing about leads and lags of the various time series do not. While the mean delay would justify classifying autJK as lagging by one period, the cross-correlation was highest for coincident data. GerGHI, for its part, would be classified as lagging by one quarter according to the frequency-domain-based method, whereas r_{max} is highest at a three-quarters lag in the time domain[108]. The largest difference between both approaches in the first-order-difference case can be observed for the German financial, real estate, renting and business services (gerJK). Whereas the mean delay indicates a lead by one-fourth of a quarter (0.21), the cross-correlation statistics suggest a lag by one year (t_{max} at minus four quarters).

For the HP-filtered data case, differences are not that large between the information about leads and lags given by cross-correlations and mean delays. None of the latter exceeds one or minus one quarter, and this is closely in line with the information provided by cross-correlations. Only in the case of gerGHI and gerJK, cross-correlations again suggests a lag of 3 or 4 quarters respectively, compared with the reference series, whereas mean delay statistics indicate only a small lag of approximately half a quarter.

The picture is similar for BK-filtered data. The signs of the period shift seem to be the same between the cross-correlation criteria and the mean delay. Every time cross-correlation suggests a lag, this is not contradicted by the mean. But the number of periods of leads and lags indicated by cross-correlations are again much higher than according to mean delays. The criterion of cross-correlation seems less than reliable. As in the HP-and BK-filtering cases t_{max} for gerJK is at a lag of four quarters, but the cross-correlation at t_0 is only marginally different from that.

---

108 Admittedly, the difference between the r_{max} of 0.18 and r_0 of 0.06 is quite small.

8.2.2 *Determination of the business cycle by a dynamic factor model approach*

Instead of determining the business cycle by the cyclical variations found in Austrian gross value added (without agriculture and forestry) as outlined before, the business cycle is now specified by the common variation found in all observed time series. This approach has already been presented in chapter 4.1.2. In order to avoid a bias caused by including time series with a definition rather close to each other, some of them have been discarded from the data pool.

Common variations are extracted out of the following series

autF: the Austrian construction sector

autCDE: the Austrian industrial sector (including mining and quarrying and electricity)

autGHI: Austrian services in trade, restaurants, transport and communication

autJK: Austrian services in financial intermediation, real estate and business activities

autGVAex: Austrian gross value added excluding agriculture and forestry

eurGDPex: euro area GDP excluding Austria and Germany

gerCDE: the German industrial sector (including mining and quarrying and electricity)

gerF: the German construction sector

gerGHI: German services in trade, restaurants, transport and communication gerGVAex: German gross value added excluding agriculture and forestry

gerJK: German services in financial intermediation, real estate and business activities

It has to be stressed again that this is a rather small set of time series as index models have been developed to reduce the cross-section dimension of time series while keeping their main variation characteristics. A justification for using such a small set has been given in chapter 4.1.2. and the results presented in the following will show that this method can work quite successfully despite this small data set.

Using the method outlined in chapter 4.1.2., two common factors have been extracted from the data set. These two factors together describe more than 60 percent of the total variation of the data set, which can be seen in *Tables A 5 a to c*. Additional factors would explain an even larger proportion, but would also raise the danger of reflecting idiosyncratic cycles. *Tables A 5 a to c* show the proportions of variation explained at different frequencies of the data set for the first 7 eigen values. In the case at hand, the spectral density matrix is evaluated for 7 frequencies over the interval $(0,\pi)$[109]. It turns out that the two factors used describe very well the total variation of the data set for all three filtering methods and over all given frequencies. In the first-order-difference case, the proportion of variance explained by the first two factors (represented here by their eigen values) exceeds 50 percent and goes up to 60 percent with BK-filtered data. An additional third common factor would explain only around 10 percent more of the total variance, which seems too little for considering it as a business cycle variation.

---

109 This high number of frequencies has been chosen in order to facilitate a proper classification of the time series as leading or lagging.

Not only the proportion of the total variation of the data set explained by the common factors, but also the proportion reflected in each time series is of interest. *Table A 7* gives for all three filtering methods the proportion of variation explained by the two common factors reflected by the respective time series. In the case of first-order-differenced data (the FOD section of *Table A 6*), both common factors are able to explain more than 70 percent of the variance of the series autGVAex, gerCDE and gerGVAex, which is quite in line with theory. However, the variation of euro area GDP excluding Austria and Germany is only explained to one-half (48 percent) by both factors. In all cases (except in the case of the Austrian financial intermediation, real estate and business service sector), the explanatory power of the common component increases by moving from the first-order-difference data to HP- and BK-filtered ones, supporting the view that idiosyncratic cycles are primarily a high-frequency phenomenon. This result can also be obtained by looking at the average over all series given in the bottom line or by forming averages over all frequencies up to the second eigen value of *Tables A 5 a to c*. In the BK-filtered data case, the common factors are capable of explaining nearly 70 percent of the variation of the euro area GDP series (again excluding Austria and Germany). Furthermore, the value for the Austrian industrial production has improved considerably to nearly 80 percent. The explanatory power of the two common factors is especially strong for those series responding typically to business cycle movements. This supports the view that the variance represented by the two common factors is close to something that can be considered as the business cycle. Furthermore, the exceptionally low values for some series like the construction industry in Austria and Germany and financial intermediation, real estate and business activities are quite in line with theory which suggests that these sectors have a low connection to the business cycle.

As the variation of the common factors represented in each of the series can be regarded as cleaning them by their idiosyncratic variations, the difference between looking at frequency-filtered series alone and series transformed by our dynamic factor model can be regarded as sector- or country-specific idiosyncratic cyclicality. The series representing the common component can be processed further in most cases like just filtered ones. *Table A 7 a to c* show for different filtering techniques cross-correlations with the reference series, both represented only by their common component variability. Again, the Austrian gross value added (without agriculture and forestry) serves as the reference series, but this time it is cleaned for all its idiosyncratic variation.

In the first-order-difference case, it can be observed that the Austrian construction industry – while exhibiting only a small part of common variation according to *Table A 6* – shows a strong co-movement with the reference series. Furthermore, nearly all series seem to be coincident with the reference cycle, which corresponds to the picture we got from the analysis carried out with just filtered series as given in *Table A 1 a*. Only two series are not found to be coincident. The first is gerJK (the German sector of financial intermediation, real estate and business services) which shows a lag of 4 quarters in the case of observing only the common component. This lag was somewhat shorter for the just filtered series (2 quarters). The second is the German trade, restaurants and transport and communication sector. Its common-component variation shows a leading behaviour of 2 quarters compared with the reference cycle, whereas it has been classified as lagging by 4 quarters in the unprocessed case. All in all, for first-order-differenced series, the common-components variations convey nearly the same picture of leads and lags.

For HP-filtered data, *Table A 7 b* reveals that all series cleaned for their idiosyncratic movements show coincident behaviour with regard to the business cycle represented by the cleaned reference series. For the uncleaned series, as shown in *Table A 1 b*, again the same picture emerges, but differences can be observed for gerGHI and gerJK, with both series classified as lagging according to their highest cross-correlations.

While results based on just filtered series were quite different for BK-filtered data as compared with the HP and the first-order-difference filter, they now look more similar to each other. In the present instance, nearly all series are classified as coincident according to their highest cross-correlations with the reference series. Only for the Austrian sector of financial intermediation, real estate and business services, the highest cross-correlation is observed for a lead of 4 quarters. This result is not confirmed in the case of uncleaned series. There, this sector has been classified as lagging like the series gerGHI and gerJK.

Figure 9: Common component and BK-filtered GVAex of Austria

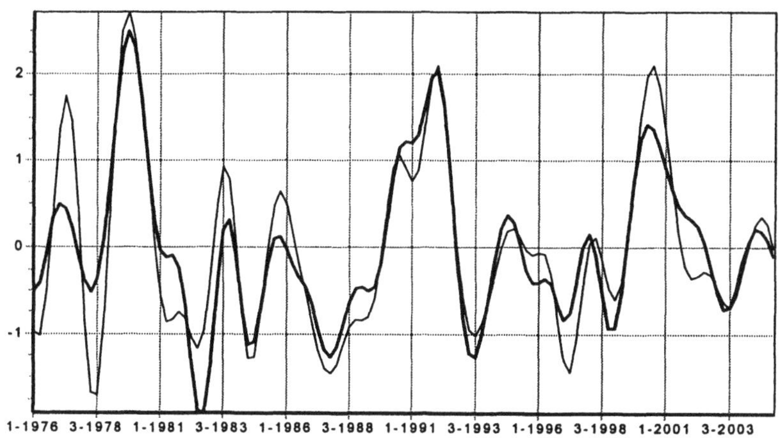

Source: Own calculations.

All in all, quite a similar picture seems to emerge when looking at leads or lags of series represented just by their common variation and the uncleaned series. Only in the case of the series gerGHI and gerJK, idiosyncratic cycles seem to matter. This result is also reflected in the case of BK-filtered data, which implies that this idiosyncratic variability has a frequency that lies within the band of business cycles (i.e. between 6 and 32 quarters). In that respect, the dynamic factor approach revealed some important information about sector-specific cyclical behaviour.

In order to give some impression of the difference between just filtered series and those filtered by the same technique, but further processed by the dynamic factor model, *Figure 9* plots both series for autGVAex, with the thin line representing just filtered values and the bold one the common component represented in this time series.

As can be observed the series just filtered for certain frequencies exhibits larger amplitudes and is not as smooth as the one represented by the common variance.

Figure 10 shows the same series, but for HP-filtered data. Again, the thin line marks the just filtered series and the bold one the common component. Again, the common component behaves more smoothly, but there seems to be no difference in amplitudes.

In both cases it becomes apparent that there are dissimilarities between the just filtered series and the one representing only its common component content. Differences show up not only in the number of peaks and troughs (and therefore of cycles), but also with regard to the dates of turning points, implying differences in leads and lags.

However, while in general the leads and lags according to the cross-correlation criterion deviate only modestly from the just filtered data set, the leading and lagging behaviour is different for the series gerGHI and gerJK, which indicates that their idiosyncratic cycles play an important role in their data generation process. Again, this can be visualised by plotting them, as given in *Figures 11* and *12*.

Figure 10: Common component and BK-filtered GVAex of Germany

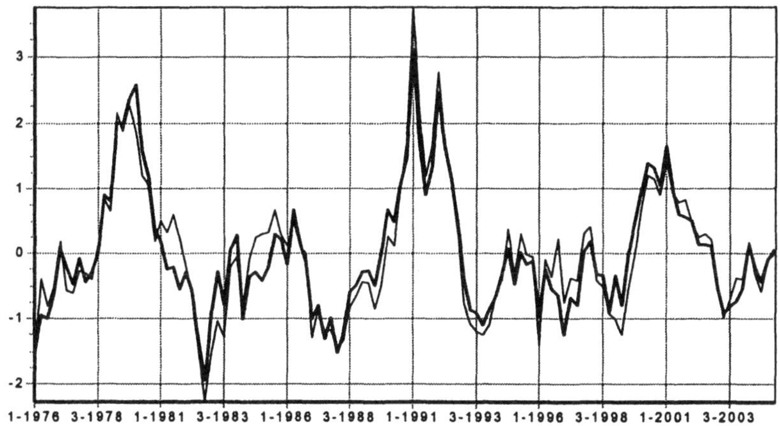

Source: Own calculations.

Figure 11: Common component and BK-filtered NACE G+H+I of Germany

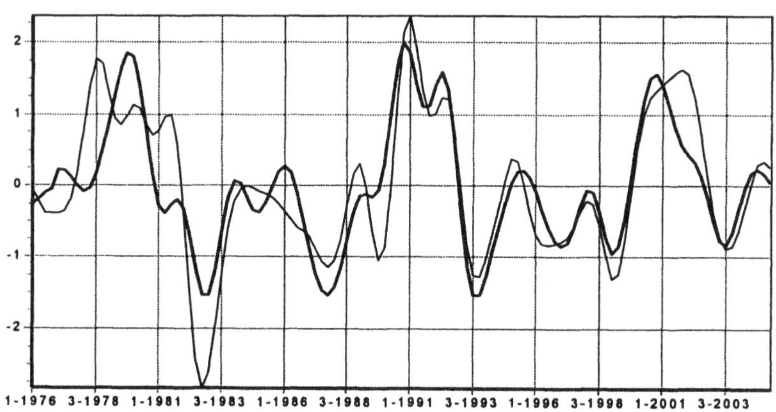

Source: Own calculations.

Figure 12: Common component and BK-filtered NACE J+K of Germany

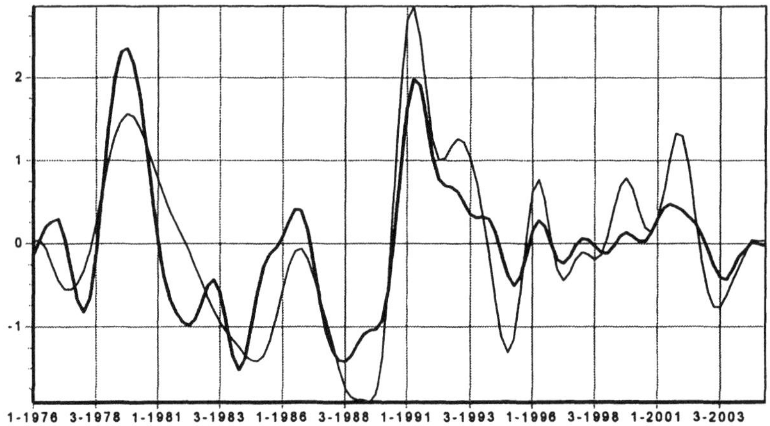

Source: Own calculations.

8.3 Dating the business cycle

8.3.1 Dating the business cycle in the ad-hoc selection framework

Figures A 1 a to A 1 c show the filtered series according all three methods with turning points indicated by small triangles. These turning points have been identified by applying the Bry-Boschan routine to all series of the three data sets. As explained in chapter 6.2., a sequence of different smoothing filters is applied, each time checking for changes in local maxima and minima. Here a Spencer curve – which is a symmetrical 2 x 7 moving average term with special weights – had been applied first, after running a procedure for detecting outliers (values deviating more than 3.5 standard deviations from the mean).

Apart from requiring consecutive turning points to show alternating signs (so that a trough has to be followed by a peak), the minimum cycle length (the time between two peaks or troughs) has been set at 6 quarters and the one for the minimum phase length (the time between two consecutive turning points of different signs) to 3 quarters. If there are two potential turning points of the same sign, only the lowest (in the case of troughs) or highest (in the case of peaks) is retained.

A further problem arises as turning points following each other have to possess different signs. Therefore, identifying the first one can be very important for estimating all following ones. As the Spencer curve smoothes the series very strongly, the first turning point was identified after applying a 2 x 4 term moving average at the beginning of the series.

Figures A 1 a to *d* show the resulting dates of the turning points for various series and different methods of cycle extraction as graphs. It can be observed that the number of turning points detected[110] varies considerably across the methods for business cycle extraction. The first-order-difference-filtered series shows the lowest number of turning points, namely 10, and their occurrence is concentrated at the beginning of the series. In the HP-filtered case, 11 turning points have been identified which are spread more or less equally over the time span. The series with the BK-filtered data shows the largest number of turning points. 15 of them have been discovered, and again they are spread more or less equally over the entire time series.

This picture seems to be stable for all different time series within the respective approach. *Figure A 1 b* shows the turning points of euro area GDP excluding Germany and Austria, and *Figure A 1 c* those of German gross value added excluding agriculture and forestry.

---

[110] A triangle pointing upwards marks a trough with its top pointing to the lowest point of the trough. Accordingly, triangles pointing downwards mark peaks.

Again, calculations on the basis of first-order-differenced data show the smallest number of turning points and of BK-filtered data the highest. Only for gerGVAex, there are two more turning points in the first-order-difference case than for HP-filtered data.

Whereas the result for leads and lags when analysing business cycle movements on the basis of cross-correlations and mean deviations seems to be rather robust over all business cycle extraction methods, things are markedly different for the dating procedure. This result is not unexpected as it seems plausible that the criteria for peaks and troughs requiring a cycle length of at least 6 quarters and a phase length of at least 3 quarters are rather hard to fulfil for time series having a large or even superimposed high-frequency variation. There are so many ups and downs in these series that a proper identification of peaks and troughs becomes a difficult task. Furthermore, it could be expected that for series with a large content of high-frequency variation, the identification of the first turning point is highly determinant for the identification of the others. Interestingly, the difference between HP- and BK-filtered data is not only marginal, as it was in the case of cross-correlations and mean delays. This time, BK-filtered data show substantially more turning points than HP-filtered ones. Again, high-frequency variations in the HP-filtered data seem to be a problem for the identification of turning points, even if they are not superimposed as in the first-order-difference case.

If one has to judge which result is most relevant for economic policy purposes, it seems to be clear that only those peaks and troughs that mark a turn in the medium (or at least not very short) term economic development are relevant. The fact that for time series including high-frequency variations the process of identification is problematic or that some of the many ups and downs may accidentally be identified as turning points, make these time series a poor guide for economic policy issues.

Figure A 1 d shows the turning points for BK-filtered data of the Austrian and German gross value added (excluding agriculture and forestry) and the euro area excluding both countries. All series start with a peak before 1978 and show nearly the same number of turning points. AutGVAex shows 15 turning points, against 14 for the two others. *Table A 2* shows the exact dates of the reference cycle's (autGVAex) turning points and the leads and lags for the other series in relation to these. The last column shows the number of extra cycles, with unfinished ones (only one peak or trough more) counting as one. As the reference cycle shows 15 turning points and eurGDPex and gerGVAex only 14, they both show one cycle less which is indicated in the last column of the respective rows.

According to this table, the Austrian business cycle (represented by the business cycle variations included in the gross value added without agriculture and forestry) recorded a peak in the second quarter of 1977. This was followed by a sharp slowdown reaching its nadir five periods later, in the third quarter of 1978. When looking at the upper part of the graph in *Figure A 1 d*, it becomes apparent that between these turning points there was a sharp drop in economic activity. This strong decline in economic activity had been identified as break in the time series and was therefore regarded as an outlier not to be classified as a turning point.

Thereafter, a strong recovery took place reaching its climax at the end of 1979. The second oil price crisis at the end of 1979 led to a period of stagnation, making it hard to find the lowest point as this cycle was tub-shaped. The Bry-Boschan procedure dates its trough in the third quarter of 1982, which seems to mark the end of the stagnation. Only one year later, the Austrian business cycle rose to a peak again, starting a series of rather short cycles. One year later, in the third quarter of 1984, economic activity again fell to a trough, swiftly followed by a peak in the fourth quarter of 1985. After overcoming the trough observed at the end of 1987, the Austrian economy started a long period of undisturbed upward movement which lasted for more than four years and ended in the first quarter of 1992. The marked recession that followed this period reached its nadir in the third quarter of 1993. The cycle following that recession peaked at the beginning of 1995. A mild recession, with its trough located in the second quarter of 1997, dampened Austrian economic activity again. Thereafter, a further business cycle set in which lasted for more than three years and peaked in the third quarter of 2000. It gave way to an extraordinary long stagnation of the Austrian economy. Over three years, activity was characterised by rather short cycles with frequencies above business cycle variations and a rather flat underlying trend. A trough in the third quarter of 2003 ended this sluggish performance and the economy re-gained momentum. For the time being, the dating procedure yields a further peak at the end of 2004, but this has to be taken with caution, as dates close to either end of the series are rather unreliable and this latest turning point is mirrored neither in euro area GDP (excluding Germany and Austria) nor in German gross value added (excluding agriculture and forestry).

Over the time span between the first quarter of 1976 and the second quarter of 2005, the Austrian economy completed all in all seven business cycles (defined as the business cycle variations found in BK-filtered Austrian gross value added), according to the Bry-Boschan dating procedure. Turning points detected in euro area GDP are plotted in the middle part of *Figure A 1 d* and their leading or lagging properties in relation to the Austrian cycle are shown in the respective row of *Table A 2*. As regards leading and lagging properties of the business cycles of the euro area and Germany, no clear picture emerges. Encouraging is, however, the small number of extra cycles for most of the observed series. This suggests that idiosyncratic cycles are of only minor importance, which is highly beneficial when setting up a dynamic factor model. Only for the sector providing financial and real estate, renting and business services and the trade, restaurant, transport and communication sector, idiosyncratic cycles seem to play a role in both countries[111].

In order to check for leads and lags of the observed time series, not only cross-correlations and mean delays are informative, but this can be done on the basis of turning points, too. In this regard, it is very helpful to calculate indicators which can give an overview about such properties. This approach is not only promising when comparing the results with the ones based on cross-correlations and coherences in view of their robustness, but has the additional advantage that leading and lagging features can also be analysed for peaks and troughs separately. *Tables A 3 a to c* show for all series their leading and lagging properties of turning points, further classified by peaks and troughs. As averages give equal weights to all values, even if they can be considered as outliers, also the median lag is reported.

Table A 3 a shows this kind of statistics for the first-order-difference case. The turning points found in the first-order-differenced series of construction industry (autF) show an average lag of 0.6 quarters *vis-à-vis* those found in the reference series (autGVAex) with the same sign. Distinguishing between peaks and troughs, peaks show an average lag of 3.2 quarters and troughs a lead of 2 quarters compared with those of the reference series. As these averages can be strongly biased by a single outlier, it is deemed appropriate to calculate a median statistic as well. Whereas the median lag of all turning points is two quarters, sign and size of medians broken down by peaks and troughs are similar to the case of averages. A different pattern of leads and lags for peaks and troughs is difficult to explain on theoretical grounds. These differences are especially pronounced in the case of first-order-differenced and

---

[111] Interestingly, GDP of Austria and Germany, like the GDP of the rest of the Euro area (eurGDPex) show one cycle less than the reference series, but total Euro Area GDP two cycles less, which is not a consistent result.

HP-filtered series. Again, this could be a hint to the difficulties arising when using time series which carry high- frequency variations.

In view of these deficiencies of first-order-differenced and HP-filtered data, the analysis of turning point sequences concentrates in the following on BK-filtered ones only. *Table A 3 c* shows average and mean leads and lags for all peaks and troughs. Euro area GDP (excluding Germany and Austria) leads the Austrian reference cycle by half a quarter on average. This goes for peaks as well as for troughs. Looking at the median shift suggests that the euro area business cycle is coincident with the Austrian cycle, with half a quarter lag for peaks and half a quarter lead for troughs.

The German business cycle – represented by the turning points *found in gross value added excluding agriculture and forestry* – shows a somewhat stronger lead *vis-à-vis* the Austrian cycle than euro area GDP[112]. Over all turning points, there exists a lead of 1.08 quarters, which is with 1.17 quarters insignificantly higher for troughs than for peaks 1.00. This result is broadly reflected by the median statistic which notes for peaks and troughs a lead of 0.5 quarters.

In line with theoretical considerations, all series representing industrial production (autCDE and gerCDE) lead the Austrian cycle, whereas German industrial production leads for peaks as well as for troughs by 0.83 quarters on average, or half a quarter in the median case. For Austrian industrial production, this lead is with 0.43 quarters in the case of averages and 0.5 for medians somewhat shorter. On average, Austrian GDP lags the cycle for peaks by approximately half a quarter, whereas it leads the cycle for troughs by the same amount of time. This yields for all turning points roughly a coincident behaviour, which is reflected by the median statistic, too.

---

[112] This implies – without prejudice to causality – that the German cycle leads the European one.

This result leads to interesting conclusions concerning the comparability of different studies on business cycles. If total production is regarded as the series representing the business cycle, then GDP as well as gross value added (in our case without agriculture and forestry) give similar results for the dates of turning points as derived by the Bry-Boschan routine. In the case of an analysis focusing on industrial production or a measure close to it, turning points are dated earlier.

The largest part of all other components – contributing to Austrian total production – shows some leading or coincident properties according to the average and the median criteria. Only autJK (the sector covering financial, real estate, renting and business services) seems to lag clearly by one quarter, with the lag in the case of troughs being somewhat higher.

For the German economy, not only the industrial sector (gerCDE) and gross value added (gerGVA and gerGVAex) lead the Austrian cycle, but also GDP as a whole seems to exhibit this property. While euro area aggregates (eurGDP and eurGDPex) show a short lead of approximately half a quarter in the case of averages, the median suggests a coincident pattern of turning points.

If we compare our leading and lagging properties found by looking at cross-correlations with those of turning points for first-order-differenced data, we are faced with inconclusive and sometimes contradicting results. This unpleasant picture is broadly confirmed in the turning point analysis comparing average and median leads and lags in *Table A 3 a*. For HP-filtered data, the situation is somewhat better but still some puzzles arise, which make a serious interpretation difficult. Thus, *Table A 1 b* shows for the German sector of trade, restaurant and transport services (gerGHI) a considerable lag of this series, according to the maximum cross-correlation as well as the mean delay criterion. Turning point analysis, however, suggests a leading behaviour for averages and medians alike.

Due to these difficulties, only results based on BK-filtered data are analysed more closely in the following. The short leading property of the euro area business cycle (excluding Germany and Austria) for averages, as shown in *Table A 3 c* (for medians only coincidence can be observed), is confirmed by cross-correlation and mean delay according to *Table A 1 c*. Looking at euro area GDP including both countries (which introduces a bias), both tables indicate a shift towards a more coincident behaviour. A different picture is presented for the German economy. Whereas *Table A 1 c* suggests a coincident behaviour of the German business cycle, represented by the series gerGVAex, with respect to the Austrian cycle, the turning point analysis in *Table A 3 c* indicates for averages and means a leading behaviour. In order to obtain a clearer picture of the German business cycle properties, the behaviour of German GDP has been observed. But looking at this series, differences become even more pronounced. Cross-correlation and mean delay statistics suggest a lag of German GDP with respect to autGVAex, while peaks and troughs are leading on average and for medians. Even the search for a possible change of the pattern over time was not successful. According to *Table A 2*, turning point dates for the first half of the series give no systematically different picture than for the second half. Therefore this question remains unresolved for the case of an ad-hoc definition of the business cycle.

The dates identified allow further the measuring of the length of cycles and phases of all series. This can be done either by simply dividing the total time span of the series of approximately 30 years by the number of cycles. For the cyclical variations included in the Austrian reference series autGVAex, this gives for seven cycles an average length of around four years for one complete business cycle. For a closer observation, *Tables A 4 a to c* show the average duration of cycles and phases, with cycles defined as the time span between two successive turning points with the same sign (two peaks or two troughs) and phases as the time span between different turning points (from peak to trough or trough to peak). Thus, two successive phases give a complete cycle. In order to capture possible asymmetries of the business cycle, spans are calculated for the time elapsed between peaks and troughs (P to T) and troughs and peaks (T to P), separately.

Due to the reasons cited above, the focus lies again on the BK- filtered data, the results of which are compared with HP- and first-order-difference-filtered data. *Table A 4 c* shows for the reference time series (autGVAex) the time elapsed between two consecutive peaks or troughs of around 15 quarters, i.e. approximately 4 years. This result contrasts the ones of the HP- and first-order-difference-filtered data, which is reproduced in *Table A 4 b* and *a*, respectively. Both show a longer cycle length of roughly 20 quarters or five years. Furthermore, they suggest an asymmetry of phases, with a time span of 12 to 13 quarters from a trough to a peak and 7 quarters from a peak to a trough. This stylised fact of longer phases of upswings than downswings is frequently reported in business cycle analysis, but is not confirmed in the BK-filter case.

In order to check, whether this kind of asymmetry is linked to the method of extraction of business cycle variations, the averages of phase and cycle length over all series are reported in the last row of the tables. Looking at the results for first-order differences, no such asymmetry seems to exist. If anything, the time elapsing from a peak to a trough, i.e. close to 11 quarters, even seems to be somewhat longer, by around 1 quarter, than the upswing phase. However, for HP filtered data, the mentioned asymmetry seems to exist. Upswing phases, with more than 12 quarters, are longer than downswings, which last less than 10 quarters. In the case of the BK filter, again no asymmetries emerge overall.

8.3.1.1 Conclusions for the ad-hoc-determined reference business cycle

The inclusion of variances higher than the frequency band of business cycles in the first-order-difference and HP-filter case yields for both data sets quite similar leading and lagging properties according to the cross-correlation criteria. Compared with BK-filtered data, only for some series where short-lived shocks (like weather conditions for instance) play a more important role, differences can be observed. Concerning the highest cross-correlations observed for various leads and lags, differences between the HP- and the BK-filtered data are minor, whereas they are substantial when compared with the first-order-differenced data.

Results of coherence estimates are quite in line with theory. Comovement with the reference series for Austria is largest for the industrial sector (autCDE) and smallest for financial intermediations services and real estate, renting and business activities (autJK). Furthermore, there is a high degree of comovement between the Austrian and the German business cycle, represented by the cyclical variation of gerGVAex (excluding agriculture and forestry), which is higher than compared with the euro area cycle (eurGDPex) and is consistent over all three filtering methods.

The calculation of shifts according to the mean delay statistics displayed much shorter leads and lags than with the maximum cross-correlation criterion. However, the signs of the shifts seem to be rather similar in the case of HP- and BK-filtered data, but not with first-order-differenced data.

The Bry-Boschan dating procedure provides different information for all three filtering methods. Not one single turning point (even if one allows for some minor shift) is the same for the first-order-difference and the HP-filter case. Only the number of turning points was nearly the same in both cases, but much higher in the case of BK-filtered data. Interestingly, for both methods showing rather erratic movements in their filtered results, fewer turning points have been detected than for the BK-filtered data. The turning point detection criteria of the Bry-Boschan procedure probably discard a lot of possible points if they are not identified with certainty.

Detecting turning points with the Bry-Boschan procedure seems to be an arbitrary procedure in the case of remaining high-frequency components. Therefore, the results based on BK-filtered data are most convincing, and some of them are mirrored in HP-filtered data. This is especially the case for German gross value added (without agriculture and forestry). Focussing on these results, the most important time series show the same number of cycles as the reference series, if we discard the last turning point of the reference series which is not reflected in other series. This reinforces the perception of a common business cycle driving the largest part of economic time series. Thus, seven cycles have been detected in the Austrian reference series, with a length of approximately 15 to 16 quarters. Phase lengths are reported to be symmetric. Mean and average distances of turning points suggest for the euro area business cycle anything between a small lead and coincident behaviour with respect to the Austrian cycle. The German business cycle, represented by business cycle variations contained in its gross value added (excluding agriculture and forestry), has been confirmed as leading by half a quarter according to mean and median distances. Industrial production of Germany shows the longest lead by one quarter, whereas Austrian industrial production leads by only half a quarter. Further robust results are a lead of the Austrian construction industry and a lag of Austrian financial intermediation, real estate, renting and business services.

8.3.2 Dating the business cycle in the dynamic factor model framework

Results are conveyed by the dates of the turning points in *Table A 8*. There, the dates are calculated by the Bry-Boschan routine, using the same settings and restrictions concerning phase, cycle length and the length of the Bartlett smoothing window as for the just cleaned series. For first-order differences, dates of turning points are the same for these two approaches till the first quarter 1980. However, the subsequent cycle is dated differently.

Looking at the results of the just filtered series, the peak following the trough at the beginning of 1980 is dated at the fourth quarter of 1981, with the following trough at the end of 1983. The equivalent peak in the common component is dated at the fourth quarter of 1982, with the following trough only at the end of 1986. No other filtering method confirms either of these turning points. For both approaches, HP-filtered data show the same date of the above-mentioned peak as a trough, whereas the subsequent cycle is dated by both approaches the same way. Again differences exist at the end of the series.

For reasons of space, observed leads and lags of turning points for all other series with respect to the reference series are not interpreted here. They can be deducted from *Table A 8* and compared with the results for just filtered series. Noteworthy seems only the fact that for turning point analysis based on common components, the number of observed extra cycles seems to be higher than for just filtered series. Obviously, the cleaning for idiosyncratic cycles did not reduce the number of turning points, but makes the common cyclicality more visible, so that it becomes easier for the Bry-Boschan algorithm to locate them.

Considering the case of BK-filtered data, the number of turning points found is the smallest. This is due to the fact, that it starts dating very late, at the beginning of 1980. Both other methods, the first-order differences and the BK filter, have already identified at least one complete cycle at that time. This interesting fact has already been observed for just filtered data in *Table A 2*. In the dynamic factor approach as well as for the just filtered data, the first turning point is a peak in the first quarter of 1980. The following trough is dated differently. In the case of just filtered data it is located at the end of 1981, whereas for the common component it occurs one year later. The following phase is dated exactly the same way, whereas the subsequent one harmonises only with respect to the year of occurrence. For the rest of the series, at least one turning point of a phase is reflected in both calendars. Again, plenty of differences can be found concerning the number of cycles of each series with respect to the reference series, but this problem seems to be less severe than when using just filtered data.

The largest difference concerning the number of dated cycles between the dynamic factor approach and just filtered data is for BK-transformed data. In the case of just filtered data, the reference series shows 15 turning points, whereas the common component of this series reports only 12. Obviously, the dynamic factor approach discarded one-and-a-half idiosyncratic cycles from the reference series autGVAex, but the dates of the remaining turning points are nearly the same. Such reduction of cycles when clearing for idiosyncratic business cycle movements is also observed for the other BK-filtered series.

The first turning point detected for both series of BK-filtered autGVAex is a peak in the second quarter of 1977, followed by a trough in the third (for just filtered series) or the second quarter (in the dynamic factor model approach) of 1978, respectively. For both approaches, the Bry-Boschan routine found the next peak in the fourth quarter of 1979 and a subsequent trough in the third or the fourth quarter of 1982, respectively. The next cycle, marked by a peak in the third quarter of 1983 and a trough in the third quarter of 1984 for just BK-filtered data, was classified as an idiosyncratic cycle by the dynamic factor model and therefore discarded, hence not showing up in the calendar of this approach.

The next peak for the common component has been detected in the third quarter of 1985 and is dated one quarter earlier for just filtered series. The end of the ensuing recession marks a trough dated at the end of 1987 for both methods. For the dynamic factor model approach, the following peak is dated in the fourth quarter of 1991 one quarter earlier than for the just filtered series (1Q1992). Again, both calendars match for the following trough that occurred in the third quarter of 1993. The subsequent recovery ended around the turn of the year 1994-1995, with the common component dating it in the last quarter of 1994 and the just filtered series at 1Q1995. Apart from the different number of cycles, the trough following that peak is the only substantial difference between both calendars. Whereas for just filtered series it is dated at the second quarter of 1997, the dynamic factor model approach locates it in the first quarter of 1999.

This is quite interesting, because usually the detection and exclusion of idiosyncratic cycles should not interfere with the dates, but just vary in their number. Looking at *Figure 8*, this difference can be explained easily by observing the amplitudes of both series. The series reflects both turns, but for the just filtered series the first turn of the second quarter of 1997 is deeper (i.e. has a higher negative amplitude) than the second in the year 1999. In the case of the dynamic factor model approach, it is the other way round and the turn of 1997 had been regarded as too local as to be classified as a trough. Obviously, the amplitude of the turn of 1997 has been magnified by an idiosyncratic component occurring at the same time.

For both approaches, the next peak was found at around the middle of 2000, where the common component dates it one quarter earlier (in the second quarter) than the just filtered series. The date of the following trough shows the same shift by one quarter. The turning point found in the common component is dated at the second quarter of 2003 and for the just filtered series at the third quarter of that year. Whereas this turning point marks the end of the calendar for series processed by the dynamic factor model approach, just filtered data show an additional phase with a peak at the end of 2004. Again, the number of extra cycles differs between both approaches for nearly all series, albeit only slightly.

In order to check the leading and lagging properties of the full set of time series in relation to the reference series, average and median leads and lags – separated by peaks and troughs – are presented in *Tables A 9 a to c* for the different filtering methods. The unclear picture that emerged for just filtered series in the case of observing first-order differences only improved slightly by clearing for their idiosyncratic cycles. *Table A 9 a* shows that there is a substantial difference between looking at average and median leads and lags, respectively. This is pointing to an unstable pattern of leads and lags, where averages are driven by extreme values. In this respect, working with data transformed by a dynamic factor model did not lead to a clearer picture.

Again, the use of HP-filtered data shows a more consistent picture for average and median leads and lags, which can probably be attributed to the lower content of high-frequency variation. But again, some ambiguous results emerged. When the results presented in *Table A 9 b* are compared with the leads and lags detected according to the cross-correlation criteria of *Table A 7 b*, it becomes apparent that medians are more similar to those. Only for autJK, the Austrian sector of financial intermediation, real estate and business services and eurGDPex, the euro area GDP (excluding Austria and Germany), turning point averages and medians are pointing to a leading behaviour, which is not confirmed if one looks only at the cross-correlations of their respective common components.

In the case of BK-filtered data, the results for averages and medians shown in *Table A 9 c* seem to be quite similar to the leading and lagging properties according to cross-correlations in *Table A 7 c*. The moments of all series are not far away from being coincident, as reflected by cross-correlations. Only for eurGDPex – the euro area GDP without Austria and Germany –, an average lead of more than one quarter is calculated, but this result is not supported by its median shift that favours a coincident behaviour. If we clear the BK-filtered data for idiosyncratic cycles, resulting turning points seem to behave quite stable as the rounded average leads and lags coincide in all but the above-mentioned case with its medians. This was not as much the case for just filtered series, as can be seen in *Table A 3 c*.

According to the results of the turning point analysis for common components with respect to the reference series based on BK-filtered data, the Austrian construction industry (autF) shows on average a small lead resulting from leads in the case of troughs, but not for peaks. Its median suggests a coincident behaviour with respect to the reference series autGVAex, but for troughs, again a lead of two quarters is observed.

The Austrian industrial sector (autCDE) exhibits a coincident behaviour which is consistent between averages and medians. For the just filtered series shown in *Table A 3 c*, a small lead can be observed.

Whereas euro area GDP (again without Austria and Germany) shows on average a lead of two quarters, which goes for peaks as well as for troughs, no such lead can be observed for the German gross value added excluding agriculture and forestry (gerGVAex). This cannot be explained by the fact that in the case of the dynamic factor estimation all series enter into the determination of the business cycle, such that business cycle dates are shifted more to an international interpretation. It is true that now also international series enter into the estimation procedure, but if they are observed for a large number of frequencies their leading and lagging properties are already considered implicitly.

Interestingly, autGHI and the German construction sector are identified as leading series, which goes for averages as well as for medians. This is not supported by theory, nor is it observed for just filtered series. The respective statistics are inconclusive, but the small lead of one quarter should not be over-emphasised. For the German trade, restaurant and transport and communication services, a small lag of one quarter is reported, whereas the just filtered results suggest a coincident behaviour. There again, no reliable conclusion can be drawn.

Tables A 10 a to c show further statistics which are similar to those presented in the *Tables A 4 a to c*. For the reference series autGVAex it can be observed that the length of cycles and phases has been reduced substantially when compared with just filtered series. This is surprising, since the clearing for idiosyncratic cycles should lead to a reduction of cycles and hence to longer cycles and phases. The reduction of variation probably allowed the Bry-Boschan routine to detect more turning points than in the case of just filtered series. This leads to a reduction of the length of cycles and phases, as can be seen in *Table A 10 a*. Now the cycle length is reduced to around 17 quarters, from around 23 quarters for just filtered series. However, this is not a general feature of the dynamic factor model output, as it is the other way round for the Austrian construction sector (autF) and for German manufacturing production (gerCDE).

The same puzzle arises when focussing on symmetries of business cycle phases. Regarding the common component, cycle phases are now more symmetric for the reference series than they were for the just filtered series. The time span of downswings (from a peak to a trough) and upswings (from a trough to a peak) is now close to nine quarters for both phases, whereas it differed substantially (7 quarters against 13 quarters) for the just filtered reference series. For other series like the Austrian construction sector (autF) and German manufacturing production (gerCDE), it is exactly the other way round: they now show more asymmetries in their cyclical behaviour.

Both facts point to a rather arbitrary dating of the cycle in the case of first-order differences. Transformation by the dynamic factor model leads to unsystematic changes of the properties of cycles when dated with the Bry-Boschan procedure. Thus, first-order differences again turn out to be an inappropriate method for the extraction of the cycle.

The same problem shows up for HP-filtered series, albeit at a smaller scale. Again, the high-frequency part included in these series leads to an unstable dating of turning points, which is reflected by the differences concerning the length of the cycle. *Table A 10 b* shows a change in the length when compared with the just filtered series given in *Table A 4 b*. Only for few series, the dates of the common components turning points show a similar cycle length. This is the case for the reference series, the German manufacturing production gerCDE and the euro area GDP (eurGDPex). Again, no systematic change of the cycle length shows up when idiosyncratic parts of the series are extracted.

For BK-filtered data, the extraction and dating of the common component did not lead to a substantial change in the length of cycles or phases. The reduced number of turning points in the common component of the reference series led to cycles becoming longer by around 3 quarters. Especially the phases of downturn (from a peak to a trough) are extended (+3 quarters), whereas for upturns only one quarter was added.

For the rest of the BK-filtered data, the picture hardly changed. In many cases, the cycle and phase lengths did not change at all. This leads to the conclusion that for the underlying data set idiosyncratic cycles are mainly a phenomenon outside the business cycle frequency band. In that case, the extraction of idiosyncratic cycles does not lead to a change in the dating calendar, but rather the different amplitude of just filtered series and common components changes the pattern of local minima and maxima.

8.3.2.1 Conclusions for the dynamic-factor-model-determined reference cycle approach

Before comparing all findings with those of other studies on the Austrian business cycle, results from this chapter are summarised. As expected, the fact that the first-order-difference filter superimposes high-frequency variations leads to a rather erratic output of the filtered series. Visual inspection does not reveal any regularity of business cycle variations. Cross-correlation statistics between the reference series and all other series are lowest for first-order difference, as included superimposed high-frequency cycles seem to be of idiosyncratic nature. The same goes for cross-correlations of common components extracted by the dynamic factor model approach. As a consequence, all other statistics checking for leads and lags of each series with respect to the reference series are of rather limited reliability. Compared with results of other approaches of filtering time series, they are not similar to any of them, whereas there is some similarity between HP- and BK-filtered data. Despite the fact that this erratic series shows a plethora of ups and downs, the criteria set in the Bry-Boschan procedure for identifying ups and downs as turning points are only rarely fulfilled such that surprisingly few turning points are detected. Nevertheless, such dating seems to be arbitrary, as a transformation by a dynamic factor model yields a completely different dating calendar. The unsystematic changes reflected by the statistics concerning the length of cycles and phases provide evidence that this dating is unreliable. Under these conditions, the extraction of a common component by a dynamic factor model approach is difficult, leading to only small explanatory power of the common component (represented by two dynamic factors) for all series.

For HP-filtered series, results are more promising. Cross-correlations for just filtered series are only marginally smaller than for BK-filtered series and give for all series the same picture of leads and lags according to the highest correlation criterion. For mean deviations calculated by (Bartlett window smoothed) cross-spectra, the picture differs somewhat, but not very much. For dynamic-factor-model-transformed series, the results are again quite similar concerning the cross-correlations for the respective series with the reference series. Only for autJK (the Austrian financial intermediation, real estate and business service sector), the cross-correlation of the common component suggests a lead of 4 quarters, whereas it shows a coincident behaviour for just filtered series.

After the application of the Bry-Boschan dating procedure, the similarities between HP- and BK-filtered data vanish. There again, the high-frequency component outside the business cycle frequency band included in HP-filtered series makes the detection of turning points a difficult and ambiguous task. Like in the case of first-order differences, only few spikes are able to pass the criteria for turning points. Therefore, the turning points given for the HP-filtered reference series differ from BK-filtered data. This automatically leads to differences in statistics relying on the detected turning points. This concerns the calculation of leads and lags and statistics indicating the lengths of cycles and phases, as well as all their averages and medians. Compared with first-order-filtered data, the transformation of HP-filtered data by the dynamic factor model also changed the turning point calendar, but this time not as much. Obviously, the inclusion of non-superimposed high-frequency data reduced this problem somewhat.

The use of band-pass-BK-filtered data turned all series to highest cross-correlation among each other. If the business cycle is defined as the common component reflected in the reference series, this result holds, too. This supports the view that the Austrian gross value added is capable of serving as a reference series. The fact that the highest cross-correlations are observed for BK-filtered data indicates that frequencies outside the business cycle band are cross-correlated to a lesser extent than frequencies within it. This is the case here, although cross-correlations only improve modestly compared with HP-filtered ones.

9. Comparing results with earlier studies on the Austrian business cycle

In this chapter, the above findings are compared with those of earlier studies on the Austrian business cycle. Some of them relate to specific sectors, some others only to the business cycle of the whole Austrian economy. There are several studies on this topic, using different methods and reference series. Only few of them focus on an explicit dating of the Austrian business cycle and none of them applies such dating on a sectoral level. Therefore no earlier study can be compared directly with the findings of the present one. Even their time horizon often differs substantially.

Despite this problem, the most relevant studies on the subject are compared with the results of this study in order to check the robustness of such dating or to give a more complete picture of the past. Some studies do not present explicit results for Austria, but only for the core of the euro area. An example is *Darvas – Szapáry* (2005) who analysed the business cycle synchronisation in the enlarged EU and therefore set up a group of countries representing the core of the EU. They compared the business cycle variations of these core countries (Austria, Belgium, France Germany, Italy and the Netherlands) with those of several different groups of central and eastern European countries. The only aspect of their studies that is of interest in this context is that among the core countries there exists a very high degree of business cycle synchronisation. This is reflected by high correlations, low volatility, small leads/lags, similar and high persistence and similar impulse-response function[113]. The following studies present more details, which makes it worth to compare each of them separately to the findings of our study. They are ordered according to the consideration they give to business cycle variations in Austria and their detail of analysis qualifying them for a comparison. In section 9.15

---

[113] See *Darvas – Szapáry* (2005), p. 27.

a summary of all dating calendars (see Table 5) of the different studies is presented.

9.1 Comparing the results with the study by *Altissimo et al.* (2001)

A rather new important study on the euro area business cycle is the one by *Altissimo et al.* (2001). They set up a dynamic factor model of 951 monthly time series starting from 1971 to the middle of 2001 in order to construct several business cycle indexes. The euro area business cycle is represented by the common component included in euro area GDP, derived by a linear interpolation of quarterly figures in order to get a monthly series. Due to data limitations, only series for the largest euro area countries like Germany, France, Italy, Spain, the Netherlands, Belgium, and – if available – for the euro area as a whole, were included. In a first step, the authors extracted business cycle frequencies out of the data set by employing a multivariate version of the band-pass filter as proposed by *Christiano – Fitzgerald* (2003). Using this filtered series, they set up a dynamic factor model, whereby the first four factors ordered by their eigen values were extracted, explaining 55 percent of the total variation within the business cycle frequency band. Given the high number of series used and their different origins, this 55 percent can be regarded as a relatively high proportion.

The authors did not address the question of synchronisation of the cyclical variations within the euro area, but focused instead on leading and lagging properties of several groups of series, like indicators of labour markets, monetary, financial and industrial conditions. They found that 258 variables show a leading property, 404 a coincident and 289 a lagging behaviour. Looking at specific countries, only Belgium and the Netherlands were classified as leading the euro area business cycle, whereas Spain and Italy lag the cycle. Their finding that the German cycle is coincident with the euro area has been confirmed only by the cross-correlation criterion of our study[114]. In our study too, the ad-hoc method as well as the dynamic-factor-model approach show their highest correlation at zero lag for the gerGVAex as well as for eurGDPex when compared with the reference series (autGVAex). But if one looks at our leading and lagging properties after dating the series by the Bry-Boschan algorithm, the picture is not so clear. Only for our band-pass-filtered series in the ad-hoc scenario, both the German as well as the euro area business cycle show approximately the same lead (*Table A 3 c*) with respect to the Austrian cycle. This leads to the conclusion that both series are coincident with each other. In the dynamic factor model approach, the same can be observed only for first-order-differenced data (*Table A 9 a*), where both series show a lag vis-à-vis the reference series. For HP- and BK-filtered data, the euro area business cycle leads the Austrian cycle, but is coincident with the German cycle (*Table A 8 b and c*).

For the euro area as a whole, *Altissimo et al.* (2001) found that industrial production is pro-cyclical with regard to the euro area business cycle. This is in line with the results found here for the manufacturing sector of Austria and Germany, represented by the variables autCDE and gerCDE. The cross-correlations presented in *Tables A 1 a to c* show – especially in the case of HP-filtered data – a coincident behaviour to the reference series autGVAex, while using just first-order-differences yields a lag and for BK-filtered data some small lead. Also the phase and cycle lengths shown in *Tables A 4 a to c* suggest that for all three filtering methods there exists a very high degree of comovement with the reference series.

As *Altissimo et al.* (2001) used a method quite similar to the dynamic factor model approach in our study, it is more appropriate to compare their results with our dynamic factor model outcome.

---

[114] As German GDP is included in the euro area with its heavy weight, this finding by *Altissimo et al.* (2001) can be regarded as being somewhat biased towards a coincident behaviour between Germany and the euro area.

In this case, the coincident behaviour of manufacturing production with the common component reflected in autGVAex is even more robust across all different filtering methods than it was in the case of using an ad-hoc definition of the business cycle.

9.2 Comparing the results with the study by *Mönch – Uhlig* (2004)

The results of the present study are only to a limited degree comparable with the study of *Mönch – Uhlig* (2004). They constructed a monthly series of euro area GDP by interpolating quarterly data using a method proposed by *Bernanke – Gertler – Watson* (1997). The interpolation has been done by regressing quarterly figures on monthly series of industrial production, retail sales, employment, etc. The authors tried to track the official NBER dating of the US cycle and the one set up by the CEPR for the euro area by applying the Bry-Boschan algorithm refined by an amplitude/phase-length criterion.

As this study concentrates entirely on the classical definition of the cycle as described in chapter 3, the number of turning points found in *Mönch – Uhlig* (2004) is clearly lower than in the present study. Nevertheless, a comparison between their dates and ours can be informative. They only identified three complete cycles. The first starts with a peak in August of 1974 and reaches a trough in April 1975. The next peak is dated at March 1980 and is followed by a trough two-and-one-half years later in July 1982. In February 1992, the peak of the last cycle was reached and the last turning point was identified for January 1993.

As time series used in this study start in 1976, only two cycle dates of the study of *Mönch – Uhlig* (2004) can be compared with ours. The peak of the euro area business cycle in March 1980 found by the authors is reflected in our HP- and BK-filter case for the univariate ad-hoc approach. In both cases, a peak is dated in the first quarter of 1980. Interestingly, the dating of first-order-differenced euro area shows a turning point with an opposite sign for the beginning of 1980, underlining its inappropriateness. In the case of our dynamic factor model approach, again the just first-order-differenced data show a trough instead of a peak for the first quarter of 1980. The common component represented in the HP-filtered euro area GDP shows a corresponding turning point in the first quarter of 1980, while BK-filtered data show it one quarter earlier, i.e. in the fourth quarter of 1979.

The end of the second cycle is dated by *Mönch – Uhlig* (2004) in the third quarter of 1982. In our ad-hoc approach, first-order-differenced euro area GDP shows no turning points around that date. However, HP-filtered data show the trough following the peak of the first quarter of 1980 for the fourth quarter of 1982 and not the third, as suggested by *Mönch – Uhlig* (2004). The BK-filtered data show it one quarter later, namely in the first quarter of 1983. For the dynamic factor model approach, the results are quite similar: no turning points around 1982 for first-order-filtered data and the same date for the trough in the fourth quarter of 1982. The BK-filtered data show now the same result as the HP series and date the trough in the fourth quarter of 1982, too.

The last cycle dated by *Mönch – Uhlig* (2004) starts with a peak in the first quarter of 1992 and a trough one year later. This is hardly supported by our data. Again, first-order-differenced data failed in both approaches to show any of these turning points. HP- and BK-filtered euro area GDP series (again without Germany and Austria) show their troughs only in the second half of 1993 and the preceding peaks already in 1990[115]. Only the common component reflected in HP-filtered euro area GDP shows a peak in the first quarter of 1992, but the subsequent trough is dated not one, but nearly two years later.

---

[115] These different results cannot be explained by different definitions of euro area GDP in both studies, because our dating calendar for Germany shows approximately the same turning points as the one for our euro area.

9.3 Comparing the results with the study by *Cheung – Westermann* (1999)

Cheung – Westermann (1999) have studied the long- and short-run relations between the Austrian and the German monthly industrial production. The long-run relation was modelled as a co-integrated vector and the short-run dynamics as deviations from long-run comovements.

The authors did not give a dating calendar from which a lead or lag relation could be deducted but instead interpret their estimated error-correction model for doing so. They found that German short-run variations (not only the ones in the business cycle frequency spectrum) lead the ones in Austria by up to two month. It is difficult to compare these findings with the ones presented here. First of all, some results of our study define the business cycle as a special range of frequencies and not only by non-trend components[116]; second, the use of monthly data does not make clear how a leading effect on a monthly basis should show up in quarterly data. If a monthly series leads the other one perfectly by one month and all turning points are located in the same respective quarter, no lead on a quarterly basis emerges. But if all turning points of the leading monthly series are located in the last month of every quarter, this leading property can also be observed on a quarterly basis. Thus, our finding of no leading property of the German business cycle or the industrial production may well be compatible with the findings of *Cheung – Westermann* (1999).

---

[116] *Fenz – Schneider* (2006) observed the comovement between Austrian and German GDP, too. Again, high- frequency variations were not filtered out hence it is difficult to compare it with the present business cycle study. Such high-frequency comovements can also be due to common events not related to the business cycle like weather conditions, etc.

9.4 Comparing the results with the study by *Brandner – Neusser* (1992)

Brandner – Neusser (1992) focused on the method of HP-filtering several macro-economic series of Austria, Germany and the US. They compared their results with other filtering methods for trend extraction, like first-order differences and exponential smoothing. Their study did not provide a dating calendar, but only cross-correlations are presented for a large set of series. Contrary to our study, *Brandner – Neusser* (1992) deduct the business cycle from quarterly GDP. Apart from the different vintages of time series in both studies, this could be a reason why cross-correlations calculated by them are somewhat lower than in the present study. Whereas they found a cross-correlation of 0.61 for HP-filtered GDP of Austria and Germany, our study gives 0.65 for just HP-filtered GVAex series. This result improves further to 0.72 if the BK filter is applied. Obviously, the frequencies above the business cycle range, included in HP-filtered series, seem to distort the true interference of the business cycle of both countries.

Concerning the leading or lagging properties of both countries' output, the authors found the highest cross-correlations for coincident series. This is quite in line with the present study and this result seems to be robust across several filtering methods[117] and is largely confirmed when looking at common components only[118].

[117] It has to be mentioned that for BK-filtered data, the German GDP lags Austrian gross value added by one period, but this deviation does not correspond to the business cycle definition here which concentrates on gross value added only.

[118] Only some results suggest a small lead of the Austrian cycle vis-à-vis the German. As *Brandner – Neusser* found that cross-correlations supporting also a small lead are not far away from their maximum for co-incident series, they favoured a leading property of Austria in their text version.

9.5 Comparing the results with the study by *Forni – Hallin – Lippi – Reichlin* (2000)

The study by *Forni et al.* (2000) is similar to the present one in that both use a dynamic factor model approach in order to identify the business cycle. The authors use a panel of 10 euro area countries, each represented by 21 macro-economic series like GDP, investment, consumption, unemployment, share prices, various monetary aggregates and price indicators, starting in 1986 and ending in 1999. Out of this data set they extracted three common factors in order to explain at least 50 percent of the total variance of the data set. As all financial and monetary variables contributed only very little to the explanation of total variance, the authors excluded them as a first step from their further analysis. They found that the common component is strongly reflected by GDP, labour market variables and incoming orders of euro area core countries (including Austria).

Forni et al. (2000) found that German GDP is not leading the euro area business cycle, represented by the common component included in euro area GDP. This result is quite in line with our findings. Apart from the just HP-filtered series in our study, this result is robust across all filtering methods and approaches to identify the cycle according the highest cross-correlation criteria, as can be seen in *Tables A 1 a to c* and *Tables A 7 a to c*.

As the authors use a very large data set, they added a lot of variance to the data set. Therefore it is clear that the common component included in the Austrian GDP explains not as much (44 percent) of the total variance of the data set as in our study (83 percent). According to their study, Austria is less influenced by the euro area business cycle than most other countries (like France, Germany, Belgium, Finland, Spain and Italy) but more than the Netherlands. Probably, this can be explained by stronger economic policy reactions in Austria in the past. Nevertheless, the Austrian business cycle is found to be coincident with the euro area cycle, like with most of the core countries.

The limited length of the data set used by *Forni et al.* (2000) led to the detection of only a few turning points. The authors did not apply a mechanical identification procedure for turning points, but dated the cycle rather by visual inspection. They found an upper turning point (start of a contraction) in the first quarter of 1990. Compared with our results for the dynamic factor model approach, this is only weakly reflected in our BK-filtered data. For this cycle, the euro area shows a lead of 5 quarters vis-à-vis the Austrian peak, dated in the fourth quarter of 1991. Our date for the start of the euro area contraction would thus be one quarter earlier than in *Forni et al.* (2000) in the fourth quarter of 1989. In the case of our just filtered series, both the HP and the BK filter dated a peak at exactly the same quarter in 1990.

The following lower turning point in the study by *Forni et al.* (2000) is found for the first quarter of 1994. Again, we found a corresponding turning point in the dynamic factor model case only for BK-filtered data, but dated two quarters earlier in 3Q1993. Interestingly, again only the HP- and BK-filtered series show a corresponding pattern. The HP-filtered series shows a trough in 3Q1993, and the BK-filtered one in 4Q1993.

The second cycle discovered by *Forni et al.* (2000) is of rather small amplitude and starts with a peak in 1Q1995. This turning point is confirmed by our study across nearly all filtering methods and approaches to determine the business cycle. The BK-filtered data show for both approaches exactly the same date for this peak. The authors date the end of this cycle by the second quarter of 1996. Our HP- and BK-filtered data date it three quarters later, first-order differenced series just filtered as well as for the dynamic factor model locate this turning point in the first quarter of 1997.

9.6 Comparing the results with the study by *Breitung – Eickmeier* (2005)

A further application of a dynamic factor model for extracting the business cycle of the European Monetary Union members (and several CEE countries) is the study conducted by *Breitung – Eickmeier* (2005). They processed a data set of 208 time series separated by blocks comprising the core EMU countries (Austria, Belgium, France, Germany, Italy, The Netherlands and Spain), the remaining EMU countries (Finland, Greece, Ireland, Luxembourg and Portugal) and eight CEECs (Czech Republic, Estonia, Hungary, Lithuania, Latvia, Poland, Slovenia and the Slovak Republic), as well as some global variables. This sample covers only ten years ranging from the first quarter of 1993 till the end of 2003. Non-stationary variables were transformed into first-order differences. Contrary to our approach, the authors applied a static factor component analysis and extracted 3 factors in order to capture the business cycle which represented 32 percent of the total variation of the data set.

Similar to the study by *Forni et al.* (2000), these three factors were able to explain 60 percent of the variation of German GDP and around 40 percent of Austrian GDP. As the aim of the study was to explore how strong these common factors were reflected by the CEEC's GDP, no lead and lag structure or a dating calendar was given.

9.7 Comparing the results with the study by *Artis – Marcellino – Proietti* (2004)

Artis – Marcellino – Proietti (2004) analysed the classical as well as the deviation business cycle of the countries that acceded to the EU in 2004 (excluding Estonia and Lithuania), 10 "old" EU Member States (including Austria) and the euro area as a whole. They used monthly series of industrial production starting 1980 at the earliest and ending in 2002 which they cleared for seasonal variations by a basic structure model approach. In order to obtain stationary time series necessary for extracting business cycle fluctuations according to the deviation cycle approach, they used two consecutively applied HP filters[119]. The following dating procedure was carried out by a Markov-switching model.

The results for the classical business cycle show that in that case the conventional wisdom of flatter business cycles in the core countries is not supported by the study of *Artis – Marcellino – Proietti* (2004). The steepness as well as the duration of recessions is much higher than those found for Germany, Italy or the euro area as a whole. This leads to bigger losses of output during recessions than in other countries.

The picture changes when one looks at the results for the deviation cycle approach. For Austria, the authors report an average duration of recessions of around 17 months, which is slightly higher than for Italy (16 months), but considerably lower than for Germany (20 months) or the whole euro area (23 months). When we compare these results with those of our study, it can be observed that the results concerning the length of recessions for first-order-differenced autCDE (which comes closest to the definition of industrial production) are much higher, irrespective of whether we concentrate only on the common component included or not. The gap is reduced by looking at HP-filtered series and shows quite similar results for BK-filtered data. This is quite plausible, because *Artis – Marcellino – Proietti* (2004) employed some kind of band-pass filter. Our HP-filtered series show a duration of economic

---

[119] As the HP-filter belongs to the class of high-pass filters, only low frequencies are filtered out. If two HP-filters with different smoothing properties are applied one after the other, they can work like a band-pass filter. Nevertheless this sort of band-pass filtering works not as exactly as the Baxter-King filter. Especially higher frequencies but still within the business cycle frequency band are erroneously filtered out, whereas high frequencies outside the band remain within the series. Therefore, the leakage of this filter is much higher than the Baxter-King filter applied in our study.

downturns (from a peak to a trough) for autCDE of somewhat below 8 quarters, which corresponds some what with the 17 months reported in *Artis – Marcellino – Proietti* (2004). This result is robust if we look at the common component only reflected in this series, which shows an average duration of 7½ quarters. For Germany and the euro area, the results are difficult to compare, as our study focuses only on gross value added excluding agriculture and forestry or GDP, respectively. Nevertheless, in the case of our just BK-filtered data, both the results for Germany and the euro area show a duration of around 8 quarters and of 20 and 23 months in the study by *Artis – Marcellino – Proietti* (2004) which corresponds quite well. The business cycle represented by the common component in the German GVAex shows a duration of 7½ quarters for recessions, which is somewhat longer than the 20 months reported in the reference study. For that approach, no euro area data including Austria and Germany have been used in order to avoid a bias, thereby inhibiting a comparison.

Artis – Marcellino – Proietti (2004) also calculated cross-correlations between countries, but only for coincident behaviour (at zero leads or lags) which can be compared with our study. *Tables A 1 a to c* show the cross-correlations calculated in our study, which show that at zero lags BK-filtered euro area GDP (including Germany and Austria) is 0.73 and for German gross value added excluding agriculture and forestry 0.72 compared with the Austrian reference series. This is somewhat lower than the values presented in *Artis – Marcellino – Proietti* (2004), who calculated for their HP band-pass deviation cycles 0.84 and 0.75, respectively, but concentrated on industrial production only[120], for which a higher comovement seems plausible.

---

[120] *Artis – Marcellino – Proietti* (2004) further calculated a so-called concordance indicator as proposed by *Harding – Pagan* (2003) which measures the fraction of time when two time series are in the same state (expansion or contraction). Interestingly, they found that this concordance between the Austrian and German industrial production is small and insignificant, whereas it is large and significant compared with the euro area. This can be interpreted such that Austrian industrial

By applying the Markov-switching model, *Artis – Marcellino – Proietti* (2004) provided a dating calendar for industrial production of all countries. Compared with our dating for the euro area by the deviation cycle approach they date the first trough in October 1993, which is rather well reflected by our results. In *Table A 2,* only first-order differences fail to show this; the BK filter dates this trough one quarter earlier in 3Q1993. Table A 7 shows that for the common component the match is even better. All filtering methods confirm this trough, but again the BK filter dates it one quarter earlier.

This trough is followed by a peak in the first quarter of 1995. For our just filtered series the results based on first-order-differences again fail to show that. HP-filtered data match only for euro area GDP without considering Austria and Germany. For the euro area as a whole, the peak is dated one quarter later in 2Q1995. In our BK-filtered case, it is the other way round: the peak in euro area GDP as a whole is dated in 1Q1995 (as it is shown by the authors with their band-pass filter), but with euro area GDP excluding Austria and Germany it is dated at 2Q1995. Using our dynamic factor model results, only euro area GDP excluding Austria and Germany is available. The first-order-differenced as well as the HP-filtered series date the corresponding peak at 2Q1995, whereas it is the same for our BK-filtered series.

The next turning point of the reference study is obtained for November 1996. The series just transformed by HP filters show the same date only for eurGDPex, but for the total euro area it is dated one quarter later. This is also the case for our BK-filtered data; both euro area aggregates show their trough in the first quarter of 1997. In the case of our dynamic factor model, again only the HP- and the BK-filtered data show a corresponding trough in the first quarter of 1997.

---

production is more closely linked to the Euro area business cycle than to the German cycle alone.

The next turning point found by *Artis – Marcellino – Proietti* (2004) is located in the first quarter of 1998 and a following trough one year later in 1Q1999. This cycle does not show up in one of our filtering techniques and business cycle determination procedures. The reason could be the small amplitude of both phases as reported by the authors. The last turning point of the reference study is a peak in the fourth quarter of 2000. This is reflected rather well by our series (except those filtered by first-order differences), but in most cases this turning point is dated one quarter earlier.

Table 3: Business cycle turning points for Austria, Germany and the euro area

	Trough	Peak	Trough	Peak	Trough	Peak	Trough
Austria	2Q1994	2Q1995	1Q1997	2Q1998	1Q1999	3Q2000	4Q2001
Germany	3Q1993	4Q1994	1Q1996	1Q1998	1Q1999	4Q2000	
Euro area	4Q1993	1Q1995	4Q1996	1Q1998	1Q1999	4Q2000	

Source: *Artis – Marcellino – Proietti* (2004).

For Germany, the authors found six turning points of the business cycle reflected by the industrial production index. Compared with our first-order-difference results as given in *Table A 2*, none of them matches. A little better is the situation for HP-filtered series. Looking at just filtered series or the ones transformed by the dynamic factor model, some of the turning points found by *Artis – Marcellino – Proietti* (2004) are mirrored in our calendar.

The closest matches are achieved with our band-pass-filtered series, which are processed in a similar way as the double HP of the authors. In the case of our just filtered series, the trough in 1993 is dated in the same quarter for gerCDE, gerGVA, gerGVAex and the German GDP. This goes also for our dynamic factor model approach with BK-filtered series. The following peak located in the fourth quarter of 1994 for just BK-filtered data is dated one quarter later in our study. The common component shows the peak for gerCDE one quarter and for gross value added 4 quarters later.

The cycle showing a trough in 1Q1996 and a peak in 1Q1998 in the study of *Artis – Marcellino – Proietti* (2004) is not mirrored in our series. Only the just HP-filtered series dates the trough exactly but misses therefore the next peak and the subsequent trough. Probably this missing cycle can be explained by its low amplitude. The trough shown for Germany in the first quarter of 1999 is confirmed by our just HP-filtered series, but it is dated one quarter later for manufacturing (gerCDE) and gross value added excluding agriculture and forestry (gerGVAex). In our dynamic factor model approach, only the BK-filtered series succeeded in dating this turning point in the same quarter.

Most interesting for our study are the turning points found by *Artis – Marcellino – Proietti* (2004) for Austria. In their study, the first trough is dated for the second quarter of 1994. This trough seems to be a false signal. None of our approaches confirms it, they date it rather around the one found by the authors for Germany and the euro area in the third or fourth quarter of 1993. The following peak of the reference study in 2Q1995 is confirmed especially well in our BK-filtered data. The dynamic factor model dates the peak of BK-filtered gross value added of the manufacturing sector (autCDE) one quarter earlier, the just BK filter approach dates it one quarter later. The next trough dated by *Artis – Marcellino – Proietti* (2004) for the first quarter of 1997 has been found only by our just BK-filtered series and the HP-filtered common component and is dated for the industrial sector at the same quarter. The following upper turning point in the second quarter of 1998 has not been indicated by any of our series.

The trough shown by the reference study for the first quarter of 1999 is only reflected by the series which did not succeed in showing the trough in the first quarter of 1997[121]. The next peak in the third quarter of 2000 is not shown in our first-order-differenced series. All other approaches confirm this turning point for the industrial sector, but only the common component of BK-filtered series dated it for the same quarter.

The last turning point found by *Artis – Marcellino – Proietti* (2004) is a trough at the end of 2001. As in the case of the first turning point, this seems to be a false signal. Again, none of our approaches confirm it, nor any results by the authors for Germany and the euro area. Apparently, the procedure for Austria has severe dating problems at either end of the series.

Nevertheless, the turning points found in the reference study are very often mirrored by one of our procedures. But the authors use a different band-pass filter which creates a higher leakage problem than our BK filter which sacrifices 6 quarters on either end of the series in order to make the filter work very exactly. It can therefore be regarded as a kind of mixture between our HP- and BK-filtering procedures. Thus, it is not surprising, that the turning points detected by the authors also seem to be a mixture of those found in our by HP- and BK-filtered series.

9.8 Comparing the results with the study by *Vijselaar – Albers* (2001)

In this study, the BK band-pass filter is applied to GDP and manufacturing production of the USA, the euro area as a whole as well separately for its Member States, Sweden and the UK. Simultaneous cross-correlations have been calculated by the authors with euro area industrial production as the reference series. The quarterly data cover the period between 1973 and 1996. In order to show the robustness of comovements, the authors additionally split

[121] This can be explained by the fact that all our procedures show one complete cycle less than the study by *Artis – Marcellino – Proietti* (2004).

the sample into two parts, one covering the period from 1979 to 1986, the other from 1987 to 1996. For the whole sample, *Vijselaar – Albers* (2001) found that euro area individual countries' manufacturing production shows a high synchronised comovement with the euro area as a whole. With regard to the size of coincident cross-correlations, Austria ranges third after France and the Netherlands. In the first period, Austria ranges second after France.

The authors further examined whether time-shifting of the data yields higher cross-correlations. With regard to manufacturing production, Austria shows a one period lag vis-à-vis the euro area, while Germany leads it by one period. This result is consistent with ours only for just BK-filtered euro area GDP excluding Germany and Austria. Our results mainly show a lag of the German economy to the euro area business cycle of one quarter, whereas total euro area GDP eurGDP (including the lagging German cycle) is coincident with the Austrian cycle.

Better comparable with our results are the ones given by *Vijselaar – Albers* (2001) for GDP series instead of industrial production. Over the whole sample period, Austrian BK-filtered GDP shows the highest simultaneous comovement with that of the euro area of all countries examined by the reference study. The comovement is especially strong in their second sub-sample covering the period between 1987 and 1996. Focussing on Austrian GDP over the whole sample period, no lead or lag can be observed, so that the Austrian business cycle shows a coincident behaviour with that of the euro area. This result is robust across both sub-samples. For the German business cycle, represented by BK-filtered GDP, the authors found again a lead of one quarter. The lag of one quarter in the first period has changed to a two-period lead in the second period. Again, this property is not supported by our findings irrespective of the filtering method and whether we look at just filtered series or their common component.

9.9 Comparing the results with the study by *Artis – Zhang* (1999)

Artis – Zhang (1999) studied the synchronisation of business cycles on the basis of OECD business cycle indicators available on a monthly basis. They used a sample of 19 countries, covering all euro area members, the USA and some other OECD countries, and ranging from 1961 to 1995. The series of Germany and the US were used as benchmark reference cycles.

The authors calculated cross-correlations separately for the pre-Exchange Rate Mechanism period of the European Monetary System (1961-1979) and the post-ERM period (after April 1979). They found that next to the Netherlands the Austrian economy showed the strongest synchronised cross-correlation with the German business cycle. Their result is robust across both periods observed.

Compared with our cross-correlation results, their results for the post-ERM period are most similar to those reflected by our BK-filtered values for gross value added without agriculture and forestry, which act as references in our study. The authors obtained a simultaneous cross-correlation of 0.78 for that period, which is rather close to our BK-filtered data (0.72). If we control for idiosyncratic cycles, as done with our dynamic factor model approach, the values surpass this cross-correlation substantially (apart from the first-order-differenced series).

9.10 Comparing the results with the study by *Dickerson – Gibson – Tsakalotos* (1998)

A further study about the closeness of correspondence of the business cycle within Europe is the one by *Dickerson – Gibson – Tsakalotos* (1998). The authors analysed HP-filtered GDP series of euro area countries as well as some others. Their data set starts in 1960 and ends in 1993 and covers GDP as well as some demand side aggregates like consumption and investment.

Based on the calculation of pair-wise cross-correlations of HP-filtered series, they conducted a cluster analysis which suggested that Belgium, France, Germany, the Netherlands, Austria, Portugal and Greece have corresponding business cycle fluctuations. For GDP, their study shows a synchronised cross-correlation between Austria and Germany of 0.74, which is somewhat above the 0.65 found for our only HP-filtered series. It is more in line with our results for BK-transformed data.

9.11 Comparing the results with the study by *Artis – Krolzig – Toro* (2004)

The study carried out by *Artis – Krolzig – Toro* (2004) is rather extensive and provides explicit dates of turning points for different EU countries. To this end, the authors used a panel of industrial production and GDP figures starting with the beginning of 1970 and ending 1996. The business cycle was identified by means of a basic structure model based on first-order-differenced data, as a unit root was found in the series. Nevertheless, the authors concentrated on the classical definition of the business cycle. In this model, there are two states of the economy incorporated. One is called "recession" and the other "expansion". Alternating between both states, with transition probabilities modelled by a Markovian-switching model, the economy is either in the strong-growth regime (expansion") or otherwise in a recession[122]. In order to capture the comovements of the business cycle states between European countries, *Artis – Krolzig – Toro* (2004) calculated a contingency table which shows the frequencies of two series being in the same state. In contrast to the vast majority of other studies, they found the highest comovement between France and Austria and Belgium and France. The simultaneous cross-correlation between Austria and Germany of the smoothed probabilities of be-

[122] For some countries, the authors modelled a third state in order to capture a structural break in the series.

ing in a recession is 0.61 over the whole sample period, which is somewhat smaller than the cross-correlation of our filtered series.

The authors reported that for Austria the average growth during a recession is –0.5 percent (compared with the previous month) and 0.11 percent for expansions. This would imply a fall in industrial production at an annualised growth rate of –5.8 percent during recessions and a rise of 1.3 percent in expansions. For Germany, an average growth rate during recessions of –0.44 percent is reported, which would imply that these fluctuations are lower than in Austria. The asymmetry of growth rates for expansions and recessions can be assigned to the authors' classical definition of the business cycle. As a consequence expansions also include trend growth biasing their growth rates downwards. Furthermore, the average time of being in a recession is rather short, with 2 quarters (7.5 months).

In order to arrive at explicit dates for the European business cycle, a multivariate Markov-switching model was set up considering industrial production and GDP, based on the same set of individual countries. For both variables the authors found only three cycles over the whole time span. Again, this is a consequence of the authors' resorting to the classical definition of the business cycle. The first cycle they found in GDP series starts with a peak in the first quarter of 1974 and has a trough in the second quarter of 1975. As this cycle is outside our time range, it can not be compared with the present study. The next peak is dated at 1Q1980 and is reflected by entire HP- and BK-filtered series; only our dynamic factor model approach dates it one quarter earlier for BK-filtered series. The following trough for the European business cycle, as reported by *Artis – Krolzig – Toro* (2004) is in 4Q1982. This time, all our methods – again apart from the ones based on first-order differences – date this turning point for exactly the same quarter. The next turning point found by the authors is a peak in 2Q1992. Again, our fist-order differences give a false signal, whereas the just HP- and BK-filtered series date this peak one quarter earlier in 1Q1992, and the same goes for the dynamic factor model results based on HP-filtered series. The common component reflected in our BK-filtered euro area GDP fails to indicate this turning point[123].

The last trough found by *Artis – Krolzig – Toro* (2004) for European GDP is in 2Q1993. Both calendars for our HP-filtered series date this trough two quarters later, whereas both approaches based on BK-filtered series date it only one quarter later in 3Q1993. First-order differences again show no meaningful results.

It is difficult to compare the turning points for the Austrian business cycle with those found by *Artis – Krolzig – Toro* (2004). For individual countries, they give no dating calendars but instead plot the probabilities for industrial production of being in either state of the business cycle. Thus, the only possibility to date them approximately is by visual inspection when results are compared to our findings for manufacturing production autCDE.

The first cycle for Austria shows a trough around the end of 1974 and a peak at the beginning of 1976. These are both located outside our sample period. The first turning point that can be compared to ours is a trough at the beginning of 1982. This turning point is reflected only by our just HP-filtered series which dates it at the last quarter of 1981. Apart from the first-order-differenced series (which again fail to give a comparable result), all other methods employed date this trough more towards the end of 1982.

The following peak identified by the authors for the Austrian business cycle is around the end of 1983. Whereas our BK-filtered series confirm this date, both procedures based on HP filters identify it one quarter later in 1Q1984. The ensuing contraction ends with a trough located around the beginning of 1986. This turning point is not reflected by our results. It is rather located in 1987 in most of our series, but for that period the authors show a peak instead. The

123 It has to be kept in mind that our definition of euro area in the case of the dynamic factor model does not comprise Austria and Germany.

last cycle matches very well with our findings. The trough in 1993 can be found in nearly all of our time series, and it is well documented by many other studies. According to *Artis – Krolzig – Toro* (2004), the last cycle ends with a peak in the middle of 1994. Apart from our badly performing fist-order- differenced series, the Bry-Boschan routine used in our study tends to date it later, at the end of 1994.

9.12 Comparing the results with the dating calendar of the CEPR

As there is no official dating of business cycle turning points for the euro area, like the one carried out by the National Bureau of Economic Research (NBER) for the US, the Centre for Economic Policy Research (CEPR) has formed an eight-member committee to set dates for the euro area. This committee has set up a chronology of recessions and expansions for the 11 original euro area member countries from 1970 to 1998 and for the current euro area as a whole since 1999.

It has chosen a definition of the business cycle similar to the NBER, but some adaptations have been made. It defines ". . . a recession as a significant decline in the level of economic activity, spread across the economy of the euro area, usually visible in two or more consecutive quarters of negative growth in GDP, employment and other measures of aggregate economic activity for the euro area as a whole, and reflecting similar developments in most countries. A recession begins just after the economy reaches a peak of activity and ends when the economy reaches its trough. Between trough and peak, the economy is formally in an expansion; between peak and trough it is in a recession. In both cases, growth rates may be low[124]." Whereas this definition explains the nature of troughs, it provides no rule for the detection of peaks.

---

124 See *CEPR* (2003).

The main differences between the approach of the NBER and the CEPR are that the latter uses quarterly data instead of monthly series. Furthermore, the business cycle reflected in individual countries plays a role in the dating procedure, too, which is not the case for the US. Seasonally adjusted GDP data seem to play the most important role for the CEPR method, without being the only ones.

This imprecise definition of the business cycle, as in the case of the NBER, leaves large room for individual interpretation. A concentration on growth rates alone (growth rate cycles) would imply that no distinction is made between trend or cycle growth rates. This reveals the adherence to the classical business cycle definition, if growth rates are not adjusted by their mean. But the CEPR stresses that looking at growth rates is not a fixed rule in its dating procedure. Nevertheless, focusing on growth rate cycles contains all the problems described in the theoretical chapter above, with the great disadvantage that the irregular component is superimposed making a reasonable dating nearly impossible. This danger is somewhat reduced by the criterion of two consecutive quarters of negative growth, but still there is no distinction between trend and business cycle growth.

As it became apparent in our calculations on the basis of first-order-differenced series, fewer turning points have been detected than with other filtering methods. Here, the reason was that the Bry-Boschan dating algorithm recognises only turning points if there is no other contradictory information in close neighbourhood. In the case of the CEPR method, the inclusion of trend growth rates shifts growth rates into the positive area, which reduces considerably the number of turning points. In this way, the concept comes closer to the classical definition of the business cycle. It is therefore not surprising that the CEPR found only three complete cycles between 1970 and 2003.

The first peak is dated at the third quarter of 1974, with a following trough in 1Q1975. This cycle is outside the period analysed in the present study and therefore cannot be compared with our findings. The next cycle starts with a peak in 1Q1980, for which our first-order-differenced series wrongly show a trough. All our other methods and approaches date this peak at the same quarter as the CEPR. Only the dynamic factor model with BK-filtered data shows it one quarter earlier in 4Q1979. The CEPR dates the next turning point for the third quarter of 1982. This trough is reflected by all our series, but it is dated one quarter later in 4Q1982. Again, results based on first-order-differenced data fail to show any reasonable result.

According to the CEPR, the next cyclical peak is located in the first quarter of 1992. With first-order-differenced data again being unable to track this, all our other approaches confirm this date. Only our dynamic factor model result for BK-filtered data of euro area GDP (excluding Germany and Austria) dates it again earlier, this time for six quarters.

The last turning point found in the CEPR calendar is a trough in the third quarter of 1993. Again, first-order differences failed. Both approaches based on BK-filtered data confirm this turning point and both based on HP-filtered data date this trough one quarter later in 4Q1993.

Interestingly, all turning points identified by the CEPR are reflected in our series, despite its focus on GDP growth rates. Obviously, the dating mechanism of the CEPR is able to locate the most conspicuous turning points, but fails to date smaller cycles. This can be seen as a direct consequence of the inclusion of trend growth which shifts growth rates upward beyond their cyclical behaviour. It is of interest whether this unequivocal set but rather scarce number of turning points is the result of the rule of two quarters of negative growth rates or whether it is obtained by the business cycle dating committee of the CEPR on the basis of external information. In order to check this, we compare our turning point dates for the euro area with those gathered solely on the basis of the rule of using two quarters of negative growth rates[125].

According to *Table 4*, euro area GDP since 1976 exhibited four periods of quarter-to-quarter negative growth rates based on seasonally adjusted series. The first recession starts in the second quarter of 1977 with a growth rate only slightly below stagnation, which is probably the reason, why this is not reflected by the CEPR dating calendar. Compared with the present study, this turning point shows up only in our two series of first-order differences, with a turning point two quarters later in 4Q1977. All our other approaches do not mirror that trough. In 2Q1980, growth rates were negative for three consecutive quarters. Again, only our first-order differences show this trough, but date it one quarter earlier in 1Q1980. Contrary to this, the CEPR as well as all our other approaches show a peak instead in 1Q1980 or at the end of 1979, respectively.

The next episode of negative growth rates started 2Q1982, with a rate close to stagnation. The CEPR dates this trough in 3Q1982 and all our approaches – apart from first-order differences, which fail again – date this by 4Q1982. When using the growth rate concept for locating turning points, this method should show some leading property, which can actually be observed in this case. Observing the next and last trough, represented by the series of five consecutive quarters of negative growth starting in 2Q1992, this property becomes apparent, too. Our dating based on BK-filtered series, as well as the CEPR dating committee dates this in 3Q1993, our HP-filtered series in 4Q1993.

Obviously, the CEPR does not strictly adhere to the negative growth rate rule for dating troughs. It probably uses additional information leading to a slight shift in the dates of the turning points into the past. Furthermore, different vintages of the GDP growth

---

125 A similar dating calendar, but for Austrian GDP, can be found in *Scheiblecker* (2002).

data set can also lead to different dates. This has not necessarily to do with revisions of GDP itself, but with the seasonal adjustment procedure. As this is usually done by an unobserved components model or some other filtering procedure (like X12-ARIMA), past values could be slightly revised with every new observation forthcoming. Such marginal revisions can easily change turning point locations, like for two of the troughs in Table 4, if growth rates are close to zero.

Table 4: Business cycle turning points for Austria, Germany and the euro area

	Eur12 GDP growth
	In Percent
Quarters	
2Q1977	–0.01
3Q1977	–0.05
2Q1980	–0.60
3Q1980	–0.19
4Q1980	–0.02
2Q1982	–0.01
3Q1982	–0.66
4Q1982	–0.02
2Q1992	–0.87
3Q1992	–0.40
4Q1992	–0.26
1Q1993	–0.39
2Q1993	–0.05

Source: Own calculations.

Apart from this shift in turning points, the use of the rule of two negative growth rates (first-order differences of logged data like in our study) for dating troughs seems to be superior to using them in combination with the Bry-Boschan routine like in our study. Nevertheless, this rule concentrates more on the classical cycle showing much fewer troughs than concepts drawing explicitly on deviation cycles.

9.13 Comparing the results with the study by *Breuss* (1984)

There are several studies focussing especially on Austrian business cycle behaviour, but covering periods which are outside our time series domain. Examples are *Tichy* (1972) and *Deistler – Schleicher* (1974), with the latter study using spectral analysis methods. Another study conducted by *Breuss* (1984) covers at least some part of the time period of our analysis. In his study, the author used a large variety of different economic time series in order to classify them by their leading, lagging and coincident behaviour in the business cycle. Among these series, also quarterly GDP and industrial production are analysed, which makes it suitable for a comparison with our findings. While in this study quarterly GDP covers the period between 1964 and 1984, the industrial production series reaches back to 1955 and serves as the reference series for determining the leads and lags.

The study by *Breuss* (1984) focuses on the deviation cycle as well as on the classical definition in order to compare the results. Unlike the present analysis, the author extracted the trend by using the "Phase-average-trend-procedure" developed by the NBER. As explained in detail in chapter 3, this method extracts a kind of local linear trend. Like in our study, the Bry-Boschan routine serves as the dating algorithm.

Largely in line with theoretical considerations, the author detected far fewer turning points for the classical approach than when using the deviation cycle concept. This is true especially for the first half of his sample, where the Austrian economy enjoyed high trend growth due to a catching-up process. For our comparison, we only focus on the deviation cycle concept used by *Breuss* (1984) and carry out this exercise only for the period overlapping in both studies.

The first peak identified by *Breuss* (1984) is dated in the last quarter of 1976. This turning point of the Austrian business cycle is reflected by our quarterly gross value added series (excluding agriculture and forestry) only for first-order differences. While our HP-filtered series fail to show this cycle, the BK-filtered ones date it two quarters later in 2Q1977. The following trough in the first quarter of 1978 is again not mirrored by our HP-filtered series; while first-order differences date this one quarter earlier, our BK-filtered dates it one quarter later in 2Q1978.

The next and last cycle shown in the overlapping period of both studies is a peak dated by *Breuss* (1984) at the beginning of 1980. Whereas our first-order-differenced series show a trough for exactly the same quarter, this time the HP-filtered data confirm this peak for the same date. Both of our approaches based on BK-filtered data date the corresponding peak one quarter earlier. *Breuss* (1984) dated the following trough in the first quarter of 1983. This matches best with our dynamic factor model approaches for HP- and BK-filtered data, but both date it one quarter earlier, i.e. in the last quarter of the previous year. In the case of just filtered series, only the BK-filtered series show this turning point, but it is dated two quarters earlier in 3Q1982. All our other approaches fail to show this trough.

It is difficult to judge which of our approaches are best comparable with the results of *Breuss* (1984). Apart from the small number of common turning points, they are matched by different approaches. If a statement is possible at all, a slightly closer matching to our BK-filtered series can be observed. This finding is supported by the fact that the length of cycles from peak to peak as well as trough to trough calculated by *Breuss* (1984) of 16 quarters each is quite close to the results for our BK-filtered data given in *Table A 4 c* with 15.5 and 16 quarters, respectively. For first-order differences and HP-filtered data, the average is around 20 quarters.

9.14 Comparing the results with the study by *Hahn – Walterskirchen* (1992)

The last study with which we want to compare our results is the one by *Hahn – Walterskirchen* (1992) for the Austrian, German and US business cycle. They used quarterly data starting from 1960 till 1992 for industrial production, GDP as well as its demand side aggregates for all three countries. De-trending was done with a basic structural model using a stochastic random-walk trend with variable drift and clearing for seasonal variations at the same time. The residual cyclical component was dated by determination of local minima and maxima. As no mechanical dating rule was used, this was done by visual inspection.

Again, we compare the turning points published by *Hahn – Walterskirchen* (1992) only for the period overlapping with ours. For Austria, the authors dated the first peak in the second quarter of 1977, which corresponds exactly with our findings for BK-filtered time series. All other approaches failed to show this turning point. The subsequent trough in the third quarter of 1978 is again mirrored only by our BK-filtering method. While the just BK-filtered GVAex series dates it in the same quarter, the dynamic factor model approach found it one quarter earlier in 2Q1978.

The next cycle starts with a peak at the beginning of 1980. Our first-order-differenced series fail again to show this turning point, whereas both approaches using HP-filtered data matched exactly. For the BK-filtered series, this peak is dated one quarter earlier at the end of 1979. The authors dated the following trough in the last quarter of 1982. This is fully confirmed by our dynamic factor model approach based on HP- and BK-filtered data (first-order differences fail to show this). With our just filtered data only the BK filter shows a matching turning point, but dates this trough one quarter earlier in 3Q1982.

According to *Hahn – Walterskirchen* (1992), the next cycle's peak was reached in 2Q1985, which again is reflected best by our BK-filtered data. While the dynamic factor model approach dates it one quarter later in 3Q1985, the just BK-filtered gross value added (without agriculture and forestry) dates it two quarters later at the end of the year. The following trough found by *Hahn – Walterskirchen* (1992) is located at the beginning of 1987 and is not confirmed by our data. Only the unreliable results based on first-order differences in the case of the dynamic factor model show this trough one quarter earlier. Most of our other methods date it approximately one year later. The last peak found in the reference study was in the second quarter of 1990. Again, the largest part of our results dates it later, this time with a lag of one-and-a-half year. Altogether, the turning points identified by *Hahn – Walterskirchen* (1992) seem to match best, if at all, with our BK-filtered data. This is probably due to the fact that both procedures clean for the high frequency irregular component.

Apart from dating the time series, the authors examined the comovement of the business cycle with that of Germany and the US. Looking at time series cross-correlations, they found some lagging property of the Austrian business cycle vis-à-vis the German cycle by one or two quarters. This effect was somewhat reduced when focussing on turning point analysis. In this case, both cycles exhibit a coincident pattern. In our calculations, no leading or lagging property of the Austrian economy based on cross-correlations could be observed. Nevertheless, theoretical considerations would suggest a positive shift of comovement in the last decade, as the Austrian economy advanced to an important producer of car parts supplied to the German automotive industry. From that perspective, a change from a previously lagging to a more coincident pattern of total gross value added seems plausible.

9.15 Comparison of the results of different dating procedures

Based on the results of the present study and the business cycle turning points reported in the literature mentioned above, Table 5 presents an overview over different dating calendars for the Austrian and the euro area business cycle.

9.15.1 *Turning point dates of the Austrian business cycle*

For the first tier of the period starting from 1964, only the studies by *Breuss* (1984) and *Hahn – Walterskirchen* (1992) provide information about possible turning point dates of the Austrian business cycle[126]. Both studies show the same number of cycles between 1964 and 1983 with quite similar dates. The largest difference between dates identified is 2 quarters at most for troughs as well as for peaks.

Concerning the present study, both methods using BK-filtered data seem to match best the findings by *Breuss* (1984) and *Hahn – Walterskirchen* (1992) for the overlapping period. This picture changes somewhat after 1985, for which period *Hahn – Walterskirchen* (1992) report quite different turning points till the end of their sample period 1991. A possible reason could be that these kinds of studies all have the problem of drawing reliable conclusions for the end of the sample period, because revisions affect especially last observations. Indeed, in the meantime several major revisions have taken place, so that GDP is nowadays defined in a different way than 15 years ago[127].

The dating of the Austrian business cycle by *Artis – Krolzig – Toro* (2004) is decisively different from other studies and results are sometimes even in contradiction to the others. According to the majority of studies, the business cycle marked a peak around the

[126] The study by Breuss gives dates starting from 1951 onwards for certain definitions of the business cycle. For technical reasons (constraints to printing), the first period is not shown here.

[127] Apart from the innovations discussed in chapter 2, one further example is software production which was not covered by the definition of production several years ago.

change of the year 1985-1986 and a trough two years later. *Artis – Krolzig – Toro* (2004) found turning points with opposite signs in the respective periods, however. The authors used a different definition of the business cycle by focussing on the classical cycle. This obviously seems to matter a lot. For economic policy, this would require a different stance.

The results by *Artis – Krolzig – Toro* (2004) deviate not so much from our findings, but show more cycles. One reason could be that our criteria for identifying turning points are more restrictive than their Markov-switching model approach.

9.15.2 Turning point dates of the euro area business cycle

In order to date the euro area business cycle, only our results based on just HP- and BK-filtered data can be compared with those of other studies, as our dynamic factor model approach does not consider the euro area as a whole, but Austria, Germany and the rest of the euro area separately. In chapter 3, this approach was justified by avoiding a bias towards a common cyclicality which could result from the large economic weight of Germany in the euro area aggregate.

The studies defining the business cycle in the classical way show fewer cycles than the others, but between them the respective results correspond quite well. Only for rather strong recessions and booms our HP- and BK-filtered results match with their findings. This is true for the peak at the beginning of 1980 and the troughs in 1982 and 1993.

The turning point dates of the CEPR seem to lead ours by some quarters in most cases. Furthermore, the authors found an extra cycle between 1997 and 1999, which was not recognised by our Bry-Boschan routine. On the other hand, the studies by *Forni et al.* (2000) and *Artis – Krolzig – Toro* (2004) show results quite similar to ours, but with leads and lags varying somewhat over time.

Table 5: Overview over different dating calendars for Austria and the euro area

	1966				1967				1968				1969				1970			
	1	2	3	4	1	2	3	4	1	2	3	4	1	2	3	4	1	2	3	4
Austria																				
HP filter																				
BK filter																				
HP Dynamic Factor model																				
BK Dynamic Factor model																				
Breuss (1984)	▲								▼									▲		
Hahn – Walterskirchen (1992)		▲							▼										▲	
Artis – Marcellino – Proietti (2004)																				
Artis – Krolzig – Toro (2004)																				
Euro area																				
HP filter																				
BK filter																				
Mönch – Uhlig (2004)																				
Forni et al. (2000)																				
Artis – Marcellino – Proietti (2004)																				
Artis – Krolzig – Toro (2004)																				
CEPR (2003)																				

	1971				1972				1973				1974				1975			
	1	2	3	4	1	2	3	4	1	2	3	4	1	2	3	4	1	2	3	4
Austria																				
HP filter																				
BK filter																				
HP Dynamic Factor model																				
BK Dynamic Factor model																				
Breuss (1984)		▼											▲						▼	
Hahn – Walterskirchen (1992)				▼									▲						▼	
Artis – Marcellino – Proietti (2004)																				
Artis – Krolzig – Toro (2004)																▼				
Euro area																				
HP filter																				
BK filter																				
Mönch – Uhlig (2004)															▲			▼		
Forni et al. (2000)																				
Artis – Marcellino – Proietti (2004)																				
Artis – Krolzig – Toro (2004)													▲					▼		
CEPR (2003)																				

	1976				1977				1978				1979				1980			
	1	2	3	4	1	2	3	4	1	2	3	4	1	2	3	4	1	2	3	4
Austria																				
HP filter																	▲			
BK filter						▲					▼					▲				
HP Dynamic Factor model																	▲			
BK Dynamic Factor model						▲					▼					▲				
Breuss (1984)						▲				▼									▲	
Hahn – Walterskirchen (1992)						▲					▼						▲			
Artis – Marcellino – Proietti (2004)																				
Artis – Krolzig – Toro (2004)	▲																			
Euro area																				
HP filter																	▲			
BK filter				▲				▼									▲			
Mönch – Uhlig (2004)																	▲			
Forni et al. (2000)																				
Artis – Marcellino – Proietti (2004)																				
Artis – Krolzig – Toro (2004)																	▲			
CEPR (2003)																				

▲ . . . peak, ▼ . . . trough.

Continuation Table 5: Overview over different dating calendars for Austria and the euro area

	1981				1982				1983				1984				1985			
	1	2	3	4	1	2	3	4	1	2	3	4	1	2	3	4	1	2	3	4
Austria																				
HP filter				▼																
BK filter							▼				▲				▼					▲
HP Dynamic Factor model								▼												
BK Dynamic Factor model								▼											▲	
Breuss (1984)									▼											
Hahn – Walterskirchen (1992)								▼											▲	
Artis – Marcellino – Proietti (2004)																				
Artis – Krolzig – Toro (2004)					▼							▲								
Euro area																				
HP filter								▼					▲							
BK filter									▼				▲					▼		
Mönch – Uhlig (2004)							▼													
Forni et al. (2000)																				
Artis – Marcellino – Proietti (2004)																				
Artis – Krolzig – Toro (2004)								▼												
CEPR (2003)																				

	1986				1987				1988				1989				1990			
	1	2	3	4	1	2	3	4	1	2	3	4	1	2	3	4	1	2	3	4
Austria																				
HP filter		▲								▼										
BK filter								▼												
HP Dynamic Factor model		▲							▼											
BK Dynamic Factor model								▼												
Breuss (1984)																				
Hahn – Walterskirchen (1992)					▼													▲		
Artis – Marcellino – Proietti (2004)																				
Artis – Krolzig – Toro (2004)	▼							▲												
Euro area																				
HP filter					▼												▲			
BK filter	▲				▼												▲			
Mönch – Uhlig (2004)																				
Forni et al. (2000)																	▲			
Artis – Marcellino – Proietti (2004)																				
Artis – Krolzig – Toro (2004)																				
CEPR (2003)													▲							

	1991				1992				1993				1994				1995			
	1	2	3	4	1	2	3	4	1	2	3	4	1	2	3	4	1	2	3	4
Austria																				
HP filter						▲						▼					▲			
BK filter					▲						▼						▲			
HP Dynamic Factor model					▲				▼							▲				
BK Dynamic Factor model				▲							▼					▲				
Breuss (1984)																				
Hahn – Walterskirchen (1992)																				
Artis – Marcellino – Proietti (2004)														▼				▲		
Artis – Krolzig – Toro (2004)											▼									
Euro area																				
HP filter												▼					▲			
BK filter											▼							▲		
Mönch – Uhlig (2004)					▲				▼											
Forni et al. (2000)													▼				▲			
Artis – Marcellino – Proietti (2004)												▼					▲			
Artis – Krolzig – Toro (2004)						▲				▼										
CEPR (2003)								▼								▲				▼

▲ . . . peak, ▼ . . . trough.

Continuation Table 5: Overview over different dating calendars for Austria and the euro area

	1996				1997				1998				1999				2000			
	1	2	3	4	1	2	3	4	1	2	3	4	1	2	3	4	1	2	3	4
Austria																				
HP filter						▼														▲
BK filter						▼													▲	
HP Dynamic Factor model													▼							▲
BK Dynamic Factor model													▼						▲	
Breuss (1984)																				
Hahn – Walterskirchen (1992)																				
Artis – Marcellino – Proietti (2004)					▼					▲			▼						▲	
Artis – Krolzig – Toro (2004)																				
Euro area																				
HP filter				▼																
BK filter					▼														▲	
Mönch – Uhlig (2004)																				
Forni et al. (2000)		▼																		
Artis – Marcellino – Proietti (2004)				▼					▲				▼							▲
Artis – Krolzig – Toro (2004)																				
CEPR (2003)								▲				▼					▲			

	2001				2002				2003				2004				2005			
	1	2	3	4	1	2	3	4	1	2	3	4	1	2	3	4	1	2	3	4
Austria																				
HP filter								▼							▲					
BK filter											▼					▲				
HP Dynamic Factor model												▼								
BK Dynamic Factor model										▼										
Breuss (1984)																				
Hahn – Walterskirchen (1992)																				
Artis – Marcellino – Proietti (2004)				▼																
Artis – Krolzig – Toro (2004)																				
Euro area																				
HP filter	▲										▼									
BK filter											▼									
Mönch – Uhlig (2004)																				
Forni et al. (2000)																				
Artis – Marcellino – Proietti (2004)																				
Artis – Krolzig – Toro (2004)																				
CEPR (2003)																				

▲ . . . peak, ▼ . . . trough.

10. Concluding remarks

The location of business cycle turning points is still an important task for economic policy decisions. They mark the points for initiating and terminating economic policy interventions targeted to smooth business cycle variations over time.

Approximately every ten years, the Austrian Institute of Economic Research publishes results on turning points relating specifically to the Austrian business cycle. Whereas business cycle theory advances only gradually over time, the methodical tool box for the extraction and evaluation of such cycles proceeds very fast. As national economies have become more and more integrated over time, the analysis of business cycles has to take such interrelations into account. Furthermore, the responsibility for monetary policy in the euro area has been delegated by its member states to the ECB, which justifies an approach to business cycles in an international context. In order to capture these interdependencies, the present study also includes Germany – Austria's largest trading partner – as well as the euro area as a whole.

It makes an important difference whether turning point analysis is carried out in real time or in retrospect. Whereas the former is important for economic policy decisions to be taken early enough to smooth the cycle, the latter is a precondition for developing a real time dating procedure. Furthermore, there is a trade-off between dating turning points at the recent time margin and the precision of their location in the past. This advises in favour of a separation of both procedures and the present study concentrates entirely on establishing a dating calendar for the past. In order to achieve reliable results, several observations at the beginning and the end of the time series were sacrificed.

To shed light on the transmission mechanism of business cycle variations, data disaggregated by sectors have been used for this study. According to *Burns – Mitchell* (1946), business cycle variations show up in different sectors of the economy. This feature had been brought to bear in our study, by defining the international business cycle according to a multivariate approach using information by sectors.

The present study starts with an overview on the specific steps to be taken for dating the business cycle. It discusses various theoretical concepts establishing the base for different approaches for extracting cyclical variations. Filter techniques in the time as well as in the frequency domain are presented beside model-based approaches with or without assuming a specific structure. Their theoretical properties, shortcomings and implications, as documented by various empirical and theoretical studies, are examined.

Based on this information, it was decided to concentrate on three filtering methods in order to clean for a trend or to extract directly periodic variations of business cycle nature: the first-order-difference filter, the Hodrick-Prescott filter and the Baxter-King bandpass filter.

In a next step, several approaches to determine the business cycle were presented. On the basis of these considerations, the univariate, popular and rather good comparable method of ad-hoc declaration of special cycles included in gross value added without agriculture and forestry as well as a multivariate interpretation derived by a dynamic factor model has been chosen for the present study. For dating the outcome, only the Bry-Boschan routine was used. Thus, a comparison of three filtering methods alternatively combined with the ad-hoc method of selection of the business cycle and a multivariate determination has been retained. All of these respective outputs have been dated by the Bry-Boschan routine, so that we obtained six dating calendars for the Austrian business cycle, including as well all other series considered.

The least reliable results are those based on data transformed by first-order differences. This method cleans only for stochastic trends of order one, which is a rather specific kind of trend. Furthermore, it has been shown that this type of filter does not only leave the rather erratically moving high frequencies above the business cycle spectrum inside but superimposes them, instead. Despite this, it has been shown that the impact of this superimposition on the detection of lead and lag structures between time series is only marginal. Results of cross-correlations and coherence statistics are just reduced in their size (and significance) compared with the other filtering methods. Only for those series where these high-frequency components themselves possibly show some cross-correlation, overall cross-correlations shifted upward. This was the case for construction, where weather conditions interfere with the production of several sectors.

Differences between HP- and BK-filtered data concerning cross-correlations and coherences were quite small. The HP filter is able to cancel out trends of deterministic or stochastic nature up to an order of four and leaves high-frequency variations above the business cycle spectrum inside, but without superimposing them. The minor difference between comovements of HP- and BK-filtered data mirrors the dominance of business cycle variations in most of our time series, so that the inclusion of high-frequency parts disturbs this picture only to a minor extent.

From a theoretical point of view, the BK filter captures best the idea of the business cycle concept. The researcher can make explicit what he or she defines as business cycle variations. For the present study, a frequency band retaining all cycles between two and eight years' length has been used. In order to filter out these frequencies rather sharply, we allowed six observations on either end of all time series to be sacrificed. In doing so, the problem of leakage (i.e. keeping frequencies outside the desired band wrongly inside and filtering correct ones out) has been reduced significantly.

Based on this method superior to the others, we found that cross-correlation[128] and coherence statistics give support for a broadly coincident behaviour of the whole set of time series. The German GDP seems to lag the Austrian gross value added (excluding agriculture and forestry), whereas the German gross value added is found to be coincident. This small lag of German GDP makes for a synchronised comovement of total euro area GDP, whereas it shows a lead when Germany and Austria are excluded from it. However, none of the results are significant for well-founded statements to be made. Interestingly, none of the series covering manufacturing leads the cycle, whereas the sector of financial intermediation and rental services (NACE J+K) of both countries show a lag, which is not in conflict with theory.

Whereas the picture of leading and lagging properties based on cross-correlations and coherences seems to be rather stable across different filtering methods, the Bry-Boschan procedure for detecting turning points reacts rather sensitively in this respect. For series where local minima and maxima are in close neighbourhood, the criteria used by this dating algorithm are getting arbitrary. In our study, this is the case for the series including high-frequency variations: the HP-filtered series and especially the first-order-differenced data. In these cases it appears that the first turning point detected in such a series is crucial for dating the others.

As an alternative to our ad-hoc determination of the series which carries the reference business cycle information, we set up a dynamic factor model. The idea behind this procedure is to find one or more common factors reflected by a large part of our observed time series – possibly shifted by different leads or lags – in order to represent a large part of the total variation of the whole data set. These common factors can be regarded as the main driving force behind all economic time series. Therefore they can be regarded

---

[128] Cross-correlations based on band-passed filtered data correspond to the concept of dynamic correlation developed by *Croux – Forni – Reichlin* (1999).

as business cycle variations. This method was originally developed to reduce the complexity of large data sets but all of them covering only a short time span. Recent research on this topic[129] has shown that a reduction in the number of time series used does not necessarily lower the quality of the output, but that a reasonably selective approach eliminating series with a high content of idiosyncratic behaviour can indeed improve the results.

In the present study, only economic data deemed to react to the business cycle have been used to set up the dynamic factor model. Furthermore, all series describing similar aggregates have been cancelled, leaving only one of them inside. This should avoid a bias of the common component towards special variations appearing in several time series. As an example, only gross value added excluding agriculture and forestry of one country has been included, but not total gross value added or GDP, too. In order to avoid a bias towards the German business cycle, only series for Austria, Germany and the euro area adjusted for both countries have been considered.

We extracted two dynamic factors on the basis of their eigen values ordered by size. With these two factors, we were able to explain more than 60 percent of the total variation of the data set. Again, results for BK-filtered data were highest (close to 70 percent), suggesting that idiosyncratic variability is an issue more important for higher frequency components. Apart from this, the pattern of highly synchronised co-moving series across all observed frequencies was confirmed by our dynamic factor model results. Only the financial intermediation and real estate service sector shows a considerable lead of four quarters vis-à-vis the Austrian business cycle.

Generally, dating the common component included in each of the time series reduces the number of cycles detected by the Bry-

---

[129] See e.g. *Boivin – Ng* (2006) or *Inklaar – Jacobs – Romp* (2003).

Boschan routine, as compared with just filtered series. This is quite in line with theory, as the dynamic factor model is used for cleaning idiosyncratic cycles. Only in the case of first-order-differenced series, the number of cycles detected increases. This can be explained by the fact that the large number of ups and downs of just first-order-filtered time series is reduced by the dynamic factor model by idiosyncratic ones. This reduction led to a lower number of local minima and maxima, making it easier for the Bry-Boschan routine to locate them.

Therefore, the BK-filter approach seems to be for theoretical as well as for practical reasons, the superior preparation for dating a cycle. Comparing the dating calendars for the Austrian business cycle of just BK-filtered series with the ones represented by their common component, one can observe that the number of cycles is lower in the latter case. A short- lived cycle reflected in just filtered Austrian gross value added (without agriculture and forestry) starting with a trough in 3Q1983 and a following peak one year later has been recognised as of idiosyncratic nature and was therefore filtered out. The absence of this cycle for that period is confirmed by all studies compared with in chapter 9. They neither show this cycle for the euro area nor for Austria[130].

There is only one further significant difference between just BK-filtered series and the ones transformed by the dynamic factor model, namely a trough following the peak around the change of the year 1994-1995. Whereas this is dated in the first case in the second quarter of 1997, it is located in the first quarter of 1999 by the common component approach. To check this again, results are compared with other studies. Unfortunately, only one of the studies presented in chapter 9 can be compared for this time span. *Artis – Marcellino – Proietti* (2004) confirm both troughs and

---

130 Only three studies provide a comparable dating calendar: *Artis – Krolzig – Toro* (2004), *Hahn – Walterskirchen* (1992) and the dating calendar for the euro area by the CEPR.

locate a peak in-between in the second quarter of 1998. Obviously, this peak is too low to be captured by our Bry-Boschan routine, hence it was ignored.

In *Figure* 9 these differences in the dating calendars are illustrated graphically. Both series show spikes of negative amplitude in the second quarter of 1997 and the first quarter of 1999. Looking at the thin line (representing just BK-filtered data), the trough in 2Q1997 is deeper than the one observed in 1Q1999. For the bold line representing the common component based on BK-filtered data, it is the other way round. Obviously, part of the amplitude in 2Q1997 has been considered as idiosyncratic. Since the Bry-Boschan routine considers within a close neighbourhood only the turning point with the largest amplitude, we get different dates for the troughs. The peak detected by *Artis – Marcellino – Proietti* (2004) in 2Q1998 is too close to the high peak in 2000, which is the reason for the Bry-Boschan routine considering it only as an intermediate turn, although it can be observed in both of our series in *Figure* 9.

If we define the business cycle as a domestic phenomenon, but accept influences from the international business cycle, then the dating calendar based on just BK-filtered series is the best choice. For those who regard the business cycle more as an international phenomenon, the dynamic factor model output is superior. If the settings prepared for our Bry-Boschan algorithm were to allow shorter cycles, also the peak described in *Artis – Marcellino – Proietti* (2004) would enter our calendars. Hence it depends on the preferences of the analyst or the economic policymaker, which calendar is most appropriate.

In general, the turning points in our study based on BK-filtered data largely correspond to the ones found when using more advanced business cycle extraction methods. Concerning the dates located by our Bry-Boschan routine, it became apparent that studies based on Markov-switching model show rather similar results.

References

Aaaland, D., "Detrending time-aggregated data", Economics Letters, 2005, (89).

Aiginger, K., Strategien zur Steigerung von Wachstum und Beschäftigung in Österreich, WIFO-Monatsberichte, 2005, 78(6).

Altissimo, F., Bassanetti, A., Cristadoro, R., Forni, M., Lippi, M., Reichlin, L., Verones, G., "EuroCOIN: A Real Time Coincident Indicator of the euro Area Business Cycle", CEPR Working Paper, 2001, (3108).

Artis, M., Krolzig, H. M., Toro, J., "The European Business Cycle", Oxford Economic Papers, Oxford University Press, 2004, 56.

Artis, M., Marcellino, M., Proietti, T., "Characterizing the Business Cycle for Accession Countries", CEPR Discussion Paper, 2004, (4457).

Artis, M., Zhang, W., "Further Evidence on the International Business Cycle and the ERM: is there a European Business Cycle?", Oxford Economic Papers, 1999, 51.

Barlevy, G., "The Cost of Business Cycles and the Benefits of Stabilization: A Survey", NBER Working Paper, 2004, (10926).

Baxter, M., King, R. G., "Measuring Business Cycles Approximate Band-Pass Filters for Economic Time Series", NBER Working Paper Series, 1995, (5022).

Bernanke, B., Gertler, M., Watson, M. Systematic Monetary Policy and the Effects of Oil Price Shocks, Brookings Papers on Economic Activity, 1997.

Beveridge, S., Nelson, C., "A new approach to decomposition of economic time series into permanent and transitory components with particular attention to measurement of the business cycle", Journal of Monetary Economics, 1981, 7.

Blanchard, O. J., Quah, D., "The Dynamic Effects of Aggregate Demand and Supply Disturbances", American Economic Review, 1989, 79, pp. 655-673.

Boehm, E. A., "A Review of Some Methodological Issues in Identifying and Analysing Business Cycles", Melbourne Institute Working Paper, 1998, (26/98).

Boivin, J., Ng, S., "Are More Data Always Better for Factor Analysis", Journal of Econometrics, Elsevier, 2006, 127(1), pp. 169-194.

Boschan, C., Ebanks, W. W., The Phase Average Trend: A new Way of Measuring Economic Growth, Proceedings of Business and Economic Statistic Section, American Statistical Association, 1978.

Brandner, P., Neusser, K., Business Cycles in Open Economies: Stylized Facts for Germany and Austria, Weltwirtschaftliches Archiv, 1992, 128(1).

Breitung, J., Eickmeier, S., "Dynamic Factor Models", Deutsche Bundesbank, Discussion Paper, Economic Studies, Series 1, 2005, (38).

Breuss, F., "Konjunkturindikatoren für die österreichische Wirtschaft", WIFO-Monatsberichte, 1984, 55(8).

Bry, G., Boschan, C., Cyclical analysis of Time Series: Selected Procedures and Computer Programs, NBER, Technical Paper, New York, 1971, (20).

Burns, A. F., Mitchell, W. C., Measuring Business Cycles, Volume 2 of Studies in Business Cycles, NBER, 1946.

Canova, F., "Detrending and Business Cycle Facts", Journal of Monetary Economics, 1998, 41.

Carvalho, V. M., Harvey, A., "Convergence and Cycles in the euro Zone", CEPR Working Paper, 2004, (4726).

Center for Economic Policy Research, Business Cycle Dating Committee of the Center for Economic Policy Research, CEPR, September 2003, http://www.cepr.org/press/dating.pdf.

Cheung, Y.-W., Westermann, F., "German Effects on the Austian Business Cycle", Weltwirtschaftliches Archiv, 1999, 135(3).

Chow, G., Lin, A. L., "Best linear unbiased Interpolation, Distribution and Extrapolation of Time Series by Related Series", The Review of Economics and Statistics, 1971, 53(4).

Christiano, L. J., Eichenbaum, M. S., "Current Real-Business-Cycle Theories and Aggregate Labour Market Fluctuations", American Economic Review, 1992, 82, pp. 430-450.

Christiano, L. J., Fitzgerald, T. J., "The Band Pass Filter", International Economic Review, 2003, (44), pp. 435-465.

Clements, M. P., Krolzig, H.-M., "Can Regime-Switching Models Reproduce The Business Cycle Features of US Aggregate Consumption, Investment and Output?", International Journal of Finance and Economics, 2004, 9, pp. 1-14.

Cogley, T., Nason, J. M., "Effects of the Hodrick-Prescott Filter on Trend and Difference Stationary Time Series: Implications of Business Cycle Research", Journal of Economic Dynamics and Control, 1995, 19, pp. 253-278.

Croux, Ch., Forni, M., Reichlin, L., "A Measure of Comovement for Economic Variables: Theory and Empirics", CEPR Discussion Paper, 1999, (2339).

Cubadda, G., "Common Cycles in Seasonal Non-stationary Time Series", Journal of Applied Econometrics, 1999, 14.

Darvas, Z., Szarpáry, G., "Business Cycle Synchronisation in the Enlarged EU", CEPR Euro Area Business Cycle Network, Discussion Paper Series, 2005, (5179).

Deistler, M., Schleicher, St., Struktur der österreichischen Industrieproduktion – Eine spektralanalytische Untersuchung, Empirica, 1974, 1.

Dellas, H., "The Informational Role of the Business Cycle", CEPR Discussion Paper, 2003, (4076).

Dickerson, A. P., Gibson, H. D., Tsakalatos, E., "Business Cycle Correspondence in the European Union", Empirica, 1998, (25), pp. 51-77.

Diebold, F. X., Rudebush, G. D., "Scoring the Leading Indicators", Special Studies Papers, Federal Reserve Board, Washington, D.C., 1987, (206).

Diebold, F. X., Senhadji, A. F., "The Uncertain Unit Root in Real GNP: Comment", The American Economic Review, 1996, 86.

Fagan, G., Henry, J., Mestre, R., "An Area Wide Model (AWM) for the euro Area", ECB Working Paper, 2001, (42).

Fenz, G., Schneider, M., Nimmt der Einfluss Deutschlands auf Österreich ab? Synchronisation und Übertragung von Konjunkturschocks, Geldpolitik und Wirtschaft, Q2/2006, Oesterreichische Nationalbank, 2006.

Fiorentini, G., Planas, Ch., Business Cycle Indicators: The Sensitivity of Generalised Dynamic Factor Models to Pre-Filtering Methods, 2003, unpublished, to be downloaded under http://www.ds.unifi.it/fiorentini/PAPERS/PREFIL2.PDF.

Forni, M., Giannone, D., Lippi, F., Reichlin, L., Openening the Black Box: Structural Factor Models versus Structural VARS, Université Libre de Bruxelles, 2004 (mimeo).

Forni, M., Hallin, M., Lippi, F., Reichlin, L., "Reference Cycles: The NBER Methodology Revisited", CEPR Discussion Paper, 2000, (2400).

Gayer, Ch., Genet, J., "Using Factor Models to Construct Composite Indicators from BCS Data – A Comparison with European Commission Confidence Indicators", European Economy, European Commission Economic Papers, 2006, (240).

Geweke, J. F., "The Dynamic Factor Analysis of Economic Time Series Models", in Aigner, D. J., Goldberger, A. S. (eds.), Latent Variables in Socio-Economic Models, Noth-Holland, Amsterdam, 1977.

Goldrian, G., Lehne, B., "Zur Approximation der Trend-Zyklus-Komponente am aktuellen Rand einer Zeitreihe", Jahrbücher für Nationalökonomie and Statistik, 1999, 219(3+4).

Gomez, V., Maravall, A., "Time Series Regression with ARIMA noise and missing Observations: Program TRAMO", European University Institute, Working Paper, Florence, 1992, (92/81.

Green, G. R., Beckman, B. A., The Composite Index of Coincident Indicators and Alternative Coincident Indexes, Survey of Current Business, June 1992.

Hahn, F., Walterskirchen, E., "Stylized Facts der Konjunkturschwankungen in Österreich, Deutschland und den USA", WIFO Working Papers, 1992, (58).

Hamilton, J. D., A new Approach to the Economic Analysis of Nonstationary Time Series and the Business Cycle, Econometrica, 1989, 57.

Hamilton, J. D., Time Series Analysis, Princeton University Press, New Jersey, Princeton, 1994.

Hansen, L. P., Sargent, T. J., "Seasonality and Approximation Errors in Rational Expectation Models", Journal of Econometrics, 1993, 55, pp. 21-55.

Harding, D., Pagan, A., "Dissecting the Cycle: A Methodological Investigation", Journal of Monetary Economics, 2002, 49(2).

Harding, D., Pagan, A., "A Comparision of Two Business Cycle Methods", Journal of Economic Dynamics and Control, 2003, 27, pp. 1681-1690.

Harvey, A. C., "Forecasting, Structural Time Series and the Kalman Filter", Cambridge University Press, Cambridge, U.K., 1989.

Hess, G. D., Iwata, S., "Measuring and Comparing Business Cycle Features", Journal of Business and Economic Statistics, 1997, 11.

Hodrick, R. J., Prescott, E., "Post-war U.S. Business Cycles: An Empirical Investigation", Carnegie Mellon Univeristy, Working Paper, 1980.

Hornstein, A., "The Business Cycle and Industry Comovement", Federal Reserve Bank of Richmond, Economic Quarterly, 2000, 86, pp. 27-48.

Inklaar, R., Jacobs, J., Romp, W., "Business Cycle Indicators: Does a Heap of Indicators Help?", University of Groningen, CCSO Working Paper, 2003, (200312).

Jäger, A., Kunst, R. M., "Seasonal Adjustment and Measuring the Persistence in Output", Journal of Applied Econometrics, 1990, 5.

Joint Research Centre of the European Commission, Busy Program: User-Manual, Tools and Practices for Business Cycle Analysis in the European Union, EC Fifth Framework Program, 1993, http://www.jrc.cec.eu.int/uasa/prj-busy.asp.

Kaiser, R., Maravall, A., "Estimation of the Business Cycle: a Modified Hodrick-Prescott filter", Spanish Economic Review, 1999, 1, 2.

King, R. G., Plosser, Ch. I., "Real Business Cycles and the Test of the Adelmans", Journal of Monetary Economics, 1994, 33, pp. 405-438.

Koopman, S. J., Harvey, A. C., Doornik, J. A., Shephard, N., STAMP: Structural Time Series Analyser; Modeller and Predictor, Timberlake Conultants, 2000.

Koopmans, T. C., "Measurement without Theory", Review of Economic Statistics, 1947, 29.

Kranendonk, H., Bonenkamp, J., Verbruggen, J., "A Leading Indicator for the Dutch Economy: Methodological and Empirical Revision of the CPB system", CPB Discussion Paper, 2004, (32).

Kydland, F. E., Prescott, E. C., "Time to Build and Aggregate Fluctuations", Econometrica, 1982, 50, pp. 1345-1370.

Long, J., Plosser, C., "Real Business Cycles", Journal of Political Economy, 1983, 91, pp. 36-69.

Lucas, R. E., Jr., "Understanding Business Cycles", in Brunner, K., Meltzer, A. H. (eds.), Stabilization of the Domestic and International Economy, Carnegie-Rochester Conference Series on Public Policy, North Holland, Amsterdam, 1977, 5, pp. 7-29.

Marcet, A., Ravn, M., "The HP-Filter in Cross-Country Comparison", CEPR Discussion Paper, 2004, (4244).

Mintz, I., "Dating Post War Business Cycles: Methods and their Application to Western Germany, 1965-67", NBER Occasional Paper, New York, 1969, (107).

Mönch, E., Uhlig, H., "Towards a Monthly Business Cycle Chronology for the euro Area", CEPR Discussion Paper, 2004, (4377).

Morley, J. C., Nelson, C. R., Zivot, E., Why Are Beveridge-Nelson and Unobserved-Component Decompositions of GDP so Different?, 2002 (mimeo), http://www.econ.washington.edu/user/cnelson/MNZ.pdf.

Neftci, F. N., "Optimal Prediction of Cyclical Downturns", Journal of Economic Dynamics and Control, 1982, 4.

Nelson, Ch., Plosser, Ch., "Trends and Random Walks in Macro-Economic Time Series: Some Evidence and Implications", Journal of Monetary Economics, 1982, 10.

Nordhaus, W. D., "The Political Business Cycle", Review of Economic Studies, 1975, 43.

Partridge, M. D., Rickman, D. S., "Regional Cyclical Symmetries in an Optimal Currency Area: An Analysis Using US State Data", Oxford Economic Papers, 2005, 75, pp. 373-397.

Peña, D., Box, G. E. P., "Identifying a Simplifying Structure in Time Series, Journal of the American Statistical Association", 1987, 82, pp. 836-843.

Prescott, E., "Theory Ahead of Business Cycle Measurement", Carnegie-Rochester Conference Series on Public Policy, 1986, 25.

Rebelo, S., "Real Business Cycle Models: Past, Present and Future", Scandinavian Journal of Economics, 2005, 107(2), pp. 217-238.

Reis, R., "The Time-Series Properties of Aggregate Consumption: Implications for the Cost of Fluctuations", NBER Working Paper, 2005, (11297).

Ritschl, A., Uebele, M., "Stock Markets and Business Cycle Comovement in Germany Before World War I: Evidence from Spectral Analysis", CEPR Discussion Paper, 2005, (5370).

Rudebusch, G. D., "The Uncertain Unit Root in Real GNP", The American Economic Review, 1993, 83.

Rünstler, G., "The long-run impact of foreign shocks to the Austrian economy: an analysis at the sectoral level", Applied Economics, 1994, 26.

Sargent, T. J., Sims, C. A., "Business Cycle Modelling Without Pretending to Have Too Much a priori Economic Theory", in Sims, C. A. (ed.), New Methods in Business Research, Federal Reserve Bank of Minneapolis, 1977.

Scheiblecker, M., "Konjunkturzyklen der österreichischen Wirtschaft", WIFO-Monatsberichte, 2002, 75(7).

Sims, C. A., "Rational Expectations Modelling with Seasonally Adjusted Data", Journal of Econometrics, 1993, 55, pp. 5-19.

Solow, R. M., "Growth Theory, New York", Oxford University Press, 1970.

Stock, J. H., Watson, M. W., "New Indexes of Coincident and Leading Economic Indicators, Macroeconomics Annual", M.I.T. Press, 1989, 4.

Stock, J. H., Watson, M. W., "A Probability Model of the Coincident Economic Indicators", in Lahiri, K., Moore, G. (eds.), Leading Economic Indicators: New Approaches and Forcasting Records, Cambridge University Press, 1991.

Stock, J. H., Watson, M. W., "Macroeconomic Forecasting using Diffusion Indexes", Journal of Business and Economic Statistics, 2002, (20), pp. 147-162

The Business Cycle Dating Committee, The NBERs Business-Cycle Dating Procedure, NBER, October 2003.

Tichy, G., Indikatoren der österreichischen Konjunktur 1950 bis 1970, WIFO-Studien und Analysen, 1972, (4).

Tichy, G., Konjunktur – Stilisierte Fakten, Theorie, Prognose, Springer Verlag, Berlin, 2. Auflage, 1994.

Tsay, R. S., "Testing and Modelling Treshold Autoregressive Processes", Journal of the American Statistical Association, 1989, 84(405), pp. 231-240.

Vijselaar, F. W., Albers, R. M., Cyclical Convergence in Europe, Kredit und Kapital, 2001, 2.

Watson, M. W., "Macroeconomic Forecasting Using Many Predictors", Princeton University Press, 2000 (mimeo).

Wecker, W., "Predicting the Turning Points of a Time Series", Journal of Business, 1979, 52, pp. 33-50.

Woitek, U., "More International Evidence on the Historical Properties of Business Cycles", Journal of Monetary Economics, 2001, 47, pp. 321-346.

Zarnowitz, V., Business Cycles – Theory, History, Indicators, and Forecasting", University of Chicago, NBER, 1992.

Zarnowitz, V., Boschan, Ch., Cyclical Indicators: An Evaluation and New Leading Indexes, Business Conditions Digest, May 1975, pp. v-xiv.

Zarnowitz, V., Moore, G. H., "Sequential signals of recession and recovery", Journal of Business, 1982, 55, pp. 57-85.

Annex

Figure A 1 a: Bry-Boschan turning points for Austrian gross value added excluding agriculture and forestry

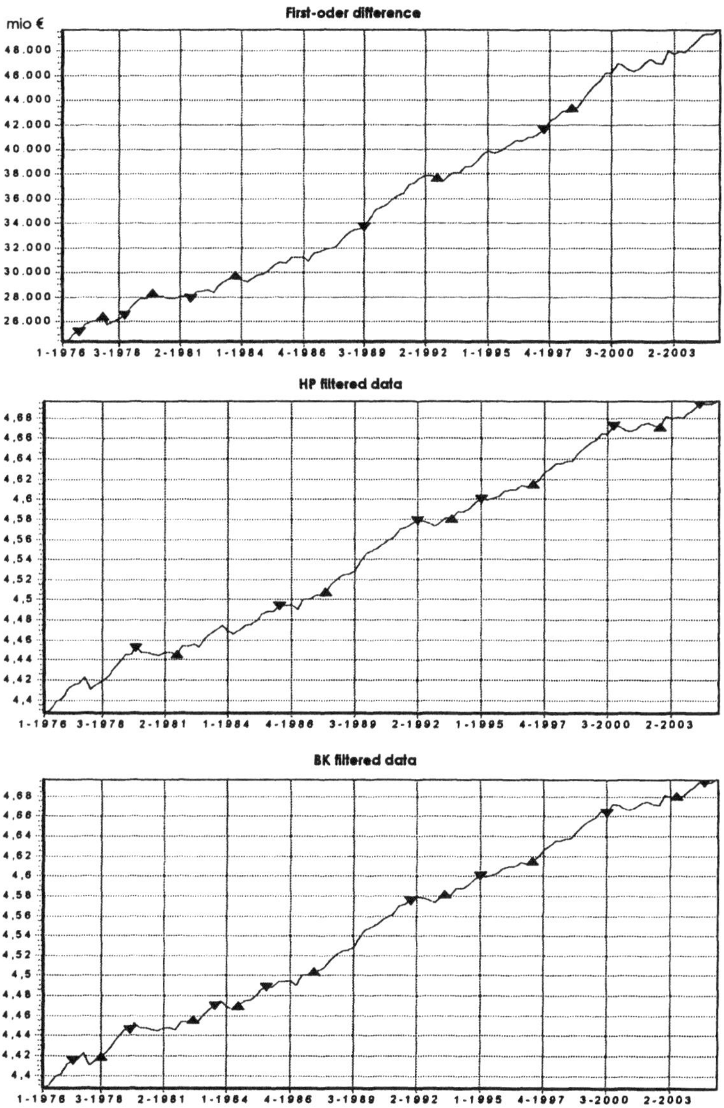

Source: Own calculations.

Figure A 1 b: Bry-Boschan turning points for euro area GDP excluding Germany and Austria

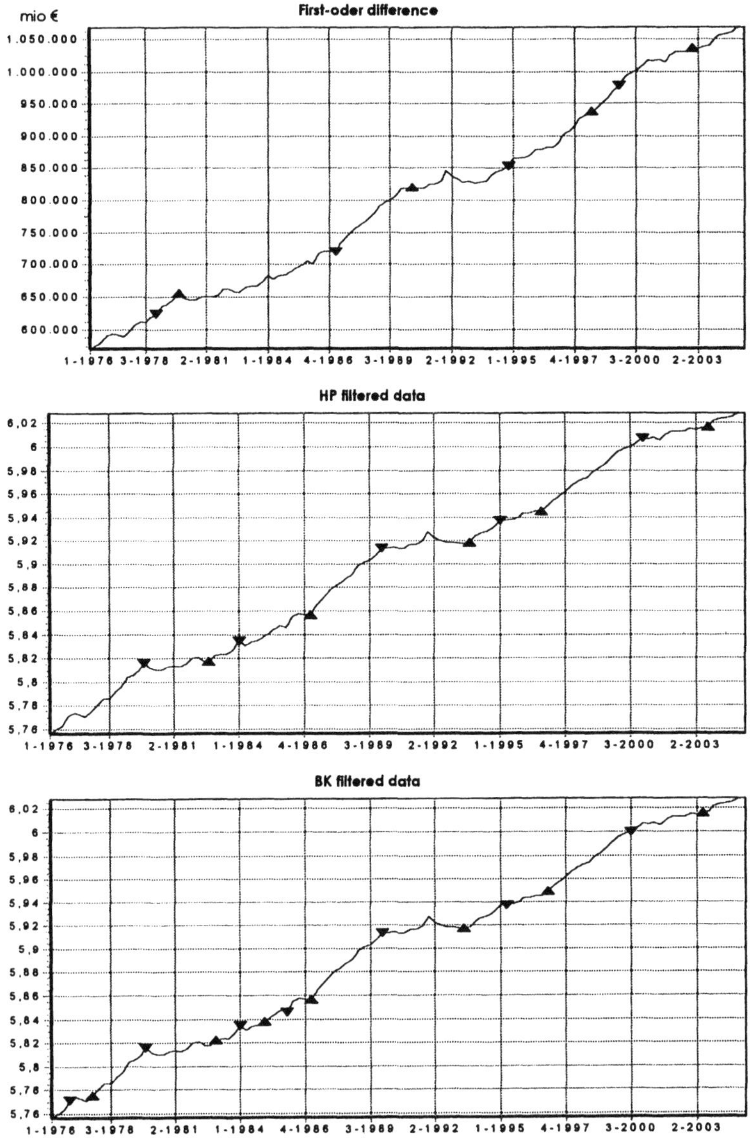

Source: Own calculations.

Figure A 1 c: Bry-Boschan turning points for German gross value added excluding agriculture and forestry

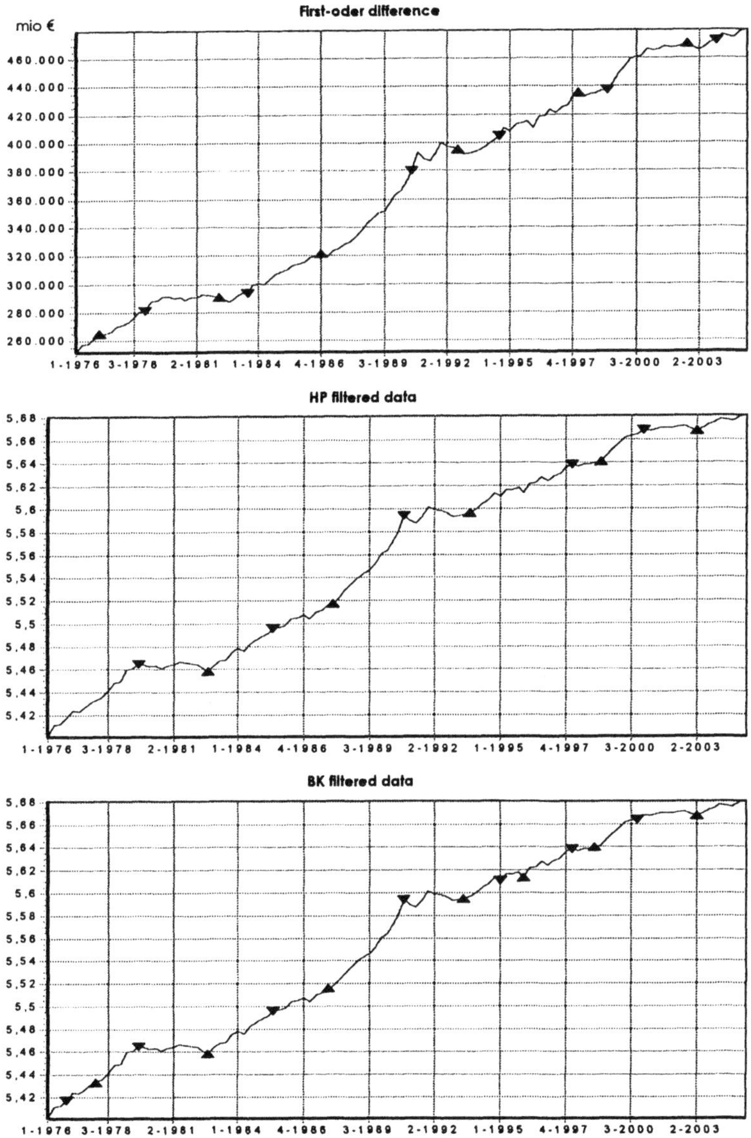

Source: Own calculations.

Figure A 1 d: Bry-Boschan turning points for different regions of BK filtered data

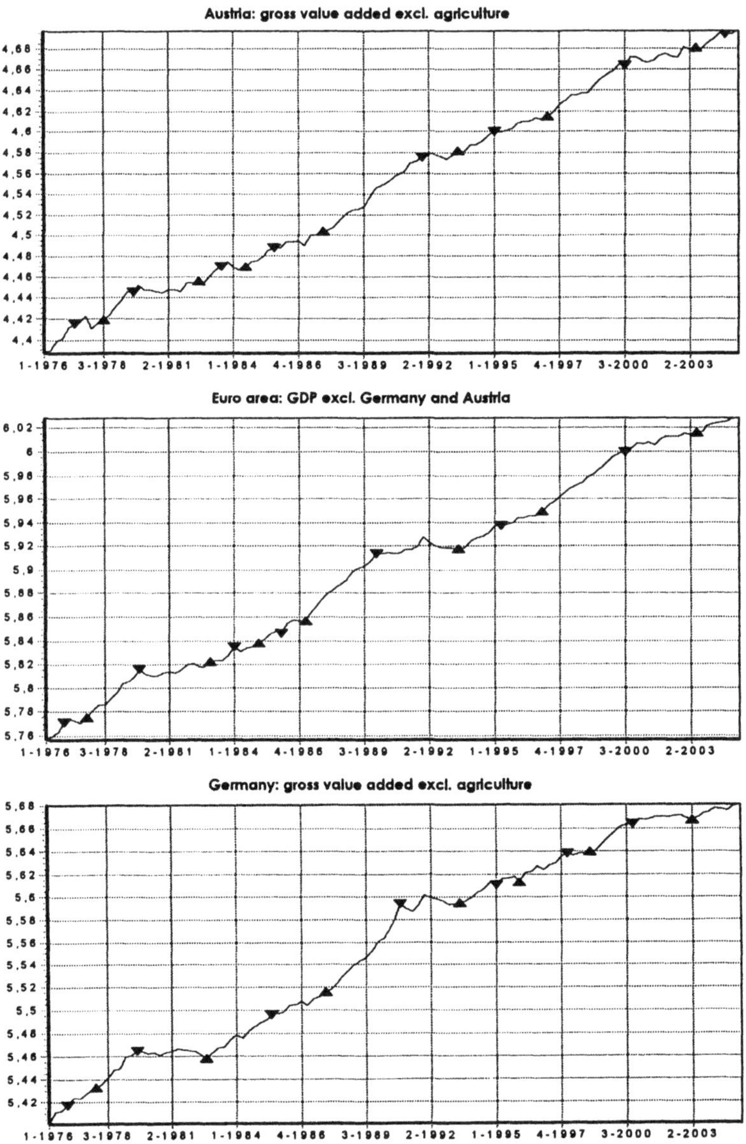

Source: Own calculations.

Table A 1 a: Bivariate statistics with the Reference Series: Austrian gross value added excluding agriculture

Series	Characteristics		Coherence	Average Spectrum	Mean Delay	Cross-correlation		
	Transf.	Freq.	6 Obs - 32 Obs	6 Obs - 32 Obs	6 Obs - 32 Obs	r_0	r_{max}	t_{max} [1]
aufF	DLX	4	0.32	0.15	0.04	0.53	0.53	0
autCDE	DLX	4	0.52	0.14	0.24	0.58	0.58	0
autGDP	DLX	4	0.69	0.19	0.09	0.77	0.77	0
autGHI	DLX	4	0.45	0.18	0.09	0.57	0.57	0
autGVA	DLX	4	0.96	0.16	0.02	0.95	0.95	0
autJK	DLX	4	0.05	0.24	-0.78	0.24	0.24	0
eurGDP	DLX	4	0.31	0.2	0.03	0.41	0.41	0
eurGDPex	DLX	4	0.24	0.18	0.1	0.36	0.36	0
gerCDE	DLX	4	0.27	0.18	0.17	0.39	0.39	0
gerF	DLX	4	0.14	0.15	0.26	0.25	0.25	0
gerGDP	DLX	4	0.17	0.2	-0.12	0.25	0.25	0
gerGHI	DLX	4	0.04	0.14	-0.74	0.06	0.18	-3
gerGVA	DLX	4	0.26	0.18	0.03	0.31	0.31	0
gerGVAex	DLX	4	0.26	0.18	0.06	0.32	0.32	0
gerJK	DLX	4	0.05	0.23	0.21	0.08	0.25	-4

[1] *The +(-) sign refers to a lead (lag) with respect to the reference series.*

Source: Own calculations.

Table A 1 b: Bivariate statistics with the Reference Series: Austrian gross value added excluding agriculture

Series	Characteristics		Coherence	Average Spectrum	Mean Delay	Cross-correlation		
	Transf.	Freq.	6 Obs - 32 Obs	6 Obs - 32 Obs	6 Obs - 32 Obs	r_0	r_{max}	t_{max} [1]
aufF	HPLX	4	0.21	0.28	0.02	0.47	0.47	0
autCDE	HPLX	4	0.72	0.31	0.09	0.79	0.79	0
autGDP	HPLX	4	0.79	0.33	0.11	0.86	0.86	0
autGHI	HPLX	4	0.54	0.32	0.13	0.7	0.7	0
autGVA	HPLX	4	0.99	0.31	0.02	0.98	0.98	0
autJK	HPLX	4	0.04	0.35	-0.11	0.19	0.19	0
eurGDP	HPLX	4	0.51	0.34	0.09	0.67	0.67	0
eurGDPex	HPLX	4	0.38	0.33	0.24	0.57	0.57	0
gerCDE	HPLX	4	0.48	0.33	0.12	0.65	0.65	0
gerF	HPLX	4	0.21	0.3	0.13	0.42	0.42	0
gerGDP	HPLX	4	0.44	0.34	-0.16	0.6	0.6	0
gerGHI	HPLX	4	0.22	0.31	-0.4	0.39	0.48	-3
gerGVA	HPLX	4	0.51	0.33	-0.08	0.65	0.65	0
gerGVAex	HPLX	4	0.5	0.33	-0.06	0.65	0.65	0
gerJK	HPLX	4	0.21	0.34	-0.31	0.39	0.53	-4

[1] *The +(-) sign refers to a lead (lag) with respect to the reference series.*

Source: Own calculations.

Table A 1 c: Bivariate statistics with the Reference Series: Austrian gross value added excluding agriculture

Series	Characteristics		Coherence	Average Spectrum	Mean Delay	Cross-correlation		
	Transf.	Freq.	6 Obs - 32 Obs	6 Obs - 32 Obs	6 Obs - 32 Obs	r_0	r_{max}	t_{max} [1]
aufF	BKLX	4	0.21	0.34	0	0.46	0.46	0
autCDE	BKLX	4	0.74	0.35	0.06	0.85	0.85	0
autGDP	BKLX	4	0.79	0.36	0.15	0.87	0.87	0
autGHI	BKLX	4	0.52	0.36	0.19	0.71	0.71	0
autGVA	BKLX	4	0.99	0.35	0.03	0.99	0.99	0
autJK	BKLX	4	0.02	0.36	-0.38	0.13	0.16	-1
eurGDP	BKLX	4	0.56	0.36	0.12	0.73	0.73	0
eurGDPex	BKLX	4	0.42	0.36	0.29	0.63	0.65	1
gerCDE	BKLX	4	0.48	0.36	0.11	0.68	0.68	0
gerF	BKLX	4	0.26	0.35	0.26	0.49	0.51	1
gerGDP	BKLX	4	0.45	0.36	-0.16	0.66	0.67	-1
gerGHI	BKLX	4	0.22	0.36	-0.43	0.44	0.55	-2
gerGVA	BKLX	4	0.54	0.36	-0.08	0.72	0.72	0
gerGVAex	BKLX	4	0.53	0.36	-0.05	0.72	0.72	0
gerJK	BKLX	4	0.2	0.36	-0.29	0.42	0.54	-4

[1] *The +(-) sign refers to a lead (lag) with respect to the reference series.*

Source: Own calculations.

Table A 2 a: Dating of turning points

FOD

	Peak	Trough	Peak	Trough	Peak	Trough	Peak	Trough	Peak	Trough	# of extra cycles
Reference Series	**Q4-1976**	**Q4-1977**	**Q4-1978**	**Q1-1980**	**Q4-1981**	**Q4-1983**	**Q3-1989**	**Q4-1992**	**Q3-1997**	**Q4-1998**	
autF	0	0	0	5	4	7	6	-15	6	-7	2
autCDE	-	0	-	-	5	14	1	-1	6	-	0
autGDP	-	-2	0	0	0	0	0	0	7	-2	2
autGHI	-	-	-	-1	4	0	2	0	-2	-2	0
autGVA	0	0	0	0	0	0	1	0	0	9	3
autJK	0	4	-	-	0	-4	-4	1	1	0	2
eurGDP	-	-	1	0	-	-	-14	-3	-2	-	-1
eurGDPex	-	-	1	0	-	-	-10	-9	9	-1	-1
gerCDE	-	0	1	2	7	12	-4	0	0	-1	2
gerF	-	-3	-1	6	8	4	-3	0	5	5	0
gerGDP	-	-	-	-	7	-6	5	0	7	-3	-1
gerGHI	3	-	-	-	7	-7	-5	0	1	-	1
gerGVA	-	-3	1	-	7	-6	5	0	7	-3	1
gerGVAex	-	-3	1	-	7	-6	5	0	7	-3	1
gerJK	-	-	-2	-	-	-5	5	4	-8	17	-1

Note: *+(-) denotes a lag (lead) with respect to the reference series.*

Remark: Positive (negative) figures give the lagging (leading) quarters of the specific series compared to to the reference series turning point dates in the first line (in bold letters). A minus indicates a missing cycle.

Source: Own calculations.

Table A 2 b: Dating of turning points

HP

Reference Series	Peak Q1-1980	Trough Q4-1981	Peak Q2-1986	Trough Q2-1988	Peak Q2-1992	Trough Q4-1993	Peak Q1-1995	Trough Q2-1997	Peak Q4-2000	Trough Q4-2002	Peak Q3-2004	# of extra cycles
aufF	2	4	-3	-5	-2	-3	-2	-6	0	0	-	1
autCDE	0	4	0	-1	-9	0	3	7	-2	2	-	0
autGDP	0	0	-	-	-3	-3	-1	0	0	0	1	-1
autGHI	-2	0	0	-1	0	-	-	-6	6	4	-	-2
autGVA	0	0	-	-	-3	0	0	0	0	0	0	-1
autJK	-9	-6	-	-5	-9	0	4	-1	0	5	-	-1
eurGDP	0	4	-	-	-1	0	1	-1	1	2	-	-2
eurGDPex	0	4	-9	-5	-9	0	0	-2	1	4	-	-1
gerCDE	-1	4	-2	-1	-5	-2	11	8	1	2	-	-1
gerF	0	3	2	-1	-9	-10	1	6	-3	1	-2	2
gerGDP	0	4	-3	-2	-5	0	-	8	-2	2	-	-1
gerGHI	-5	4	-3	-3	-	0	-1	-5	4	5	-	-1
gerGVA	-1	4	-3	-1	-5	0	-1	-5	1	2	-	0
gerGVAex	-1	4	-3	-1	-5	0	-	8	1	2	-	-1
gerJK	-1	12	1	4	-5	5	-	-	4	2	-	-2

Note: *+(-) denotes a lag (lead) with respect to the reference series.*

Remark: Positive (negative) figures give the lagging (leading) quarters of the specific series compared to to the reference series turning point dates in the first line (in bold letters). A minus indicates a missing cycle.

Source: Own calculations.

Table A 2 c: Dating of turning points

BK

	Peak	Trough	Peak	Trough	Peak	Trough	Peak	Trough	Peak	Trough	Peak	Trough	Peak	Trough	Peak	# of extra cycles
Reference Series	**Q2-1977**	**Q3-1978**	**Q4-1979**	**Q3-1982**	**Q3-1983**	**Q3-1984**	**Q4-1985**	**Q4-1987**	**Q1-1992**	**Q3-1993**	**Q1-1995**	**Q2-1997**	**Q3-2000**	**Q3-2003**	**Q4-2004**	
autF	1	1	1	-	-	0	-1	-5	-1	-3	-1	1	-1	5	-4	0
autCDE	-1	-1	1	0	1	1	1	-1	-6	0	2	-1	-1	-1	-	-1
autGDP	-	-	0	-1	0	0	0	-1	0	0	5	0	0	-1	-1	-1
autGHI	-	-	-1	-4	0	1	4	0	0	0	-2	-7	-1	0	-	-1
autGVA	0	-1	0	-1	0	1	0	0	0	0	0	0	0	0	0	0
autJK	2	6	-	-	-5	-	-	-2	1	1	4	1	0	2	-	-2
eurGDP	-2	-3	1	1	-	-	1	-2	0	0	0	-1	0	0	-	-2
eurGDPex	-2	-3	1	2	2	2	1	-3	-8	0	1	-1	0	0	-	-1
gerCDE	-1	-1	0	1	-	-	-1	0	-4	0	0	-4	1	-1	-	-1
gerF	-2	-2	-1	0	2	5	5	1	1	-1	-2	6	-3	-2	-3	1
gerGDP	-	-	1	1	-	-	-1	0	-4	0	0	-4	1	-1	-1	-1
gerGHI	5	-7	-	1	4	-	-	0	-4	1	0	-3	5	0	-	-2
gerGVA	-2	-2	0	1	-	-	0	0	0	0	0	-5	1	-1	-	-1
gerGVAex	-2	-2	0	1	-	-	-1	0	-4	0	0	-5	1	-1	-	-1
gerJK	-	-5	0	-	-	2	4	7	-3	6	5	0	-3	-1	-	-2

Note: *+(-) denotes a lag (lead) with respect to the reference series.*
Remark: Positive (negative) figures give the lagging (leading) quarters of the specific series compared to to the reference series turning point dates in the first line (in bold letters). A minus indicates a missing cycle.
Source: Own calculations.

Table A 3 a: Analysis of turning point sequences with respect to the reference series Austrian gross value added excluding agriculture

FOD

	Average Lag at			Median Lag at		
w.r.t Reference Series	**Peaks**	**Troughs**	**All**	**Peaks**	**Troughs**	**All**
aufF	3.2	-2	0.6	2	-3.5	2
autCDE	4	4.33	4.17	3	-0.5	3
autGDP	1.75	1.4	1.56	0	0	0
autGHI	1.33	-0.75	0.14	0	-0.5	-0.5
autGVA	0.2	1.8	1	0	0	0
autJK	-0.75	0.25	-0.25	0	0.5	0
eurGDP	-5	-1.5	-3.6	-8	-1.5	-2.5
eurGDPex	0	-3.33	-1.67	-4.5	-5	-0.5
gerCDE	1	2.6	1.89	0.5	0	0
gerF	-2.75	2.4	0.11	-2	2	-0.5
gerGDP	6.33	-3	1.67	6	-4.5	2.5
gerGHI	1.5	-3.5	-0.17	2	-3.5	0.5
gerGVA	5	-3	1	6	-3	0.5
gerGVAex	5	-3	1	6	-3	0.5
gerJK	-1.67	5.33	1.83	-5	-0.5	1

Note: *+(-) denotes a lag (lead) with respect to the reference series.*
Source: Own calculations.

Table A 3 b: Analysis of turning point sequences with respect to the reference series Austrian gross value added excluding agriculture

HP

	Average Lag at			Median Lag at		
w.r.t Reference Series	**Peaks**	**Troughs**	**All**	**Peaks**	**Troughs**	**All**
aufF	-1	-2	-1.5	-2	-4	-2
autCDE	-1.6	2.4	0.4	-1	1	0
autGDP	-0.6	-0.75	-0.67	-0.5	0	0
autGHI	1	-0.75	0.13	0	-0.5	0
autGVA	-0.6	0	-0.33	0	0	0
autJK	-3.5	-1.4	-2.33	-4.5	-3	-3
eurGDP	0.25	1.25	0.75	0.5	1	0.5
eurGDPex	-3.4	0.2	-1.6	-4.5	-1	0
gerCDE	0.8	2.2	1.5	-1.5	0.5	0
gerF	-1.83	-0.2	-1.09	-1	0	-0.5
gerGDP	-2.5	2.4	0.22	-2.5	1	-1
gerGHI	-1.25	0.2	-0.44	-2	-1.5	-2
gerGVA	-1.8	0	-0.9	-2	-0.5	-1
gerGVAex	-2	2.6	0.56	-2	1	-0.5
gerJK	-0.25	5.75	2.75	0	4.5	3

Note: *+(-) denotes a lag (lead) with respect to the reference series.*
Source: Own calculations.

Table A 3 c: Analysis of turning point sequences with respect to the reference series
Austrian gross value added excluding agriculture

BK

w.r.t Reference Series	**Average Lag at**			**Median Lag at**		
	Peaks	**Troughs**	**All**	**Peaks**	**Troughs**	**All**
aufF	-0.86	-0.17	-0.54	-1	0.5	-1
autCDE	-0.43	-0.43	-0.43	0	-1	-0.5
autGDP	0.57	-0.5	0.08	0	-0.5	0
autGHI	0	-1.67	-0.83	-0.5	0	0
autGVA	0	-0.14	-0.07	0	0	0
autJK	0.4	1.6	1	0.5	1	1
eurGDP	0	-0.83	-0.42	0	-0.5	0
eurGDPex	-0.71	-0.43	-0.57	0.5	-0.5	0
gerCDE	-0.83	-0.83	-0.83	-0.5	-0.5	-0.5
gerF	-0.38	1	0.27	-1.5	-0.5	-1
gerGDP	-0.67	-0.8	-0.73	-0.5	-0.5	-0.5
gerGHI	2	-1.33	0.18	2	0	0
gerGVA	-0.17	-1.17	-0.67	0	-0.5	0
gerGVAex	-1	-1.17	-1.08	-0.5	-0.5	-0.5
gerJK	0.6	1.5	1.09	-1.5	1	0

Note: *+(-) denotes a lag (lead) with respect to the reference series.*
Source: Own calculations.

Table A 4 a: Analysis of cycles with respect to the reference cycle of the Austrian gross value added excluding agriculture

FOD

Phases and cycles average duration</TH< TR>				
	P to T	**P to P**	**T to P**	**T to T**
Reference Series	**7**	**20**	**13.25**	**20.25**
autF	9.43	16.5	7	16.5
autCDE	11.5	20	11.6	23.75
autGDP	7.5	15.83	8.71	15
autGHI	8.75	20.75	12.6	22.5
autGVA	8	14	6.86	14.67
autJK	7.29	14.5	7.67	14
eurGDP	14.5	23.33	12.67	30
eurGDPex	11.5	27	16.67	30
gerCDE	8.5	15.5	7.43	14.67
gerF	14.25	23.75	9.4	22.25
gerGDP	12.67	20.33	7.5	20.33
gerGHI	10.5	15.4	7.6	15.8
gerGVA	12.4	19.2	7.67	19.8
gerGVAex	12.4	19.2	7.67	19.8
gerJK	16.25	22.33	11.33	26.67
Average	**10.78**	**19.23**	**9.73**	**20.37**

Source: Own calculations.

Table A 4 b: Analysis of cycles with respect to the reference cycle of the Austrian gross value added excluding agriculture

HP

Phases and cycles average duration</TH< TR>				
	P to T	**P to P**	**T to P**	**T to T**
Reference Series	**7.6**	**18.8**	**12**	**20.25**
autF	6.14	14.5	9.5	15.17
autCDE	10.33	17.8	8.6	19.4
autGDP	7.75	24	17	27.33
autGHI	9	29.67	20.33	28.67
autGVA	8.25	23.75	16.25	27.33
autJK	12.2	22.25	9.8	21.2
eurGDP	8.5	27.33	19.67	26.67
eurGDPex	11.2	20.25	9.75	20.25
gerCDE	9	20.5	12.25	19.75
gerF	8.14	14.57	7.29	15.83
gerGDP9	.6	19.5	11.25	19.75
gerGHI	11.6	22.25	10.4	21.2
gerGVA	8.67	16.2	8.4	15.6
gerGVAex	9.4	20.5	11.75	19.75
gerJK	13.25	28.67	13	25.5
Average	**9.41**	**21.28**	**12.33**	**21.48**

Source: Own calculations.

Table A 4 c: Analysis of cycles with respect to the reference cycle of the Austrian gross value added excluding agriculture

BK

Phases and cycles average duration</TH< TR>				
	P to T	**P to P**	**T to P**	**T to T**
Reference Series	**7.86**	**14.86**	**7.86**	**15.83**
autF	7.13	14.14	7.43	14
autCDE	7.86	14.67	8.33	15.83
autGDP	7	15.67	9.5	16
autGHI	5.14	14.5	10	13.83
autGVA	7.71	14.86	8	16
autJK	10	17.4	8.33	17.5
eurGDP	7.67	18.2	12.2	19.8
eurGDPex	8.14	15	8.33	16.33
gerCDE	8	15	8.17	15.83
gerF	8.25	12.75	5.38	13.43
gerGDP	8.17	15.5	8.17	15.6
gerGHI	9.67	17.8	8.17	17
gerGVA	7	15.17	9.5	16
gerGVAex	7.71	15.17	8.67	16
gerJK	10.17	16.8	7.17	16.5
Average	**7.97**	**15.47**	**8.45**	**15.97**

Source: Own calculations.

Table A 5 a: Proportion of power

First-order differences

Eigen value #	Frequency							
	0	**2Pi/15**	**2 * 2Pi/15**	**3 * 2Pi/15**	**4 * 2Pi/15**	**5 * 2Pi/15**	**6 * 2Pi/15**	**7 * 2Pi/15**
1	0.49	0.442	0.389	0.332	0.358	0.318	0.273	0.306
2	0.643	0.612	0.573	0.568	0.556	0.521	0.497	0.517
3	0.778	0.729	0.707	0.671	0.658	0.65	0.65	0.66
4	0.845	0.832	0.787	0.756	0.751	0.748	0.76	0.755
5	0.896	0.895	0.852	0.823	0.816	0.828	0.841	0.83
6	0.931	0.93	0.902	0.881	0.871	0.877	0.884	0.883
7	0.957	0.957	0.939	0.923	0.911	0.919	0.923	0.925

Source: Own calculations.

Table A 5 b: Proportion of power

HP

Eigen value #	**Frequency**							
	0	**2Pi/15**	**2 * 2Pi/15**	**3 * 2Pi/15**	**4 * 2Pi/15**	**5 * 2Pi/15**	**6 * 2Pi/15**	**7 * 2Pi/15**
1	0.546	0.535	0.498	0.428	0.369	0.402	0.41	0.349
2	0.659	0.654	0.638	0.608	0.573	0.564	0.549	0.52
3	0.743	0.749	0.749	0.72	0.668	0.669	0.66	0.64
4	0.821	0.827	0.832	0.805	0.751	0.748	0.747	0.745
5	0.888	0.891	0.893	0.87	0.822	0.817	0.825	0.826
6	0.931	0.931	0.93	0.909	0.879	0.873	0.88	0.878
7	0.961	0.961	0.958	0.944	0.92	0.921	0.924	0.92

Source: Own calculations.

Table A 5 c: Proportion of power

BK

Eigen value #	Frequency							
	0	2Pi/15	2 * 2Pi/15	3 * 2Pi/15	4 * 2Pi/15	5 * 2Pi/15	6 * 2Pi/15	7 * 2Pi/15
1	0.566	0.532	0.462	0.464	0.577	0.454	0.57	0.513
2	0.679	0.669	0.634	0.653	0.699	0.597	0.69	0.649
3	0.765	0.772	0.761	0.762	0.802	0.718	0.783	0.762
4	0.841	0.856	0.859	0.839	0.876	0.832	0.867	0.847
5	0.897	0.915	0.919	0.894	0.927	0.891	0.917	0.903
6	0.937	0.948	0.95	0.935	0.952	0.931	0.947	0.942
7	0.966	0.971	0.968	0.963	0.973	0.961	0.971	0.966

Source: Own calculations.

Table A 6 : Ratio common component variance over series variance

FOD

Serie Name	Ratio Value
autGVAex	0.779
aufF	0.471
autCDE	0.501
autGHI	0.494
autJK	0.312
eurGDPex	0.480
gerCDE	0.746
gerF	0.334
gerGHI	0.663
gerGVAex	0.868
gerJK	0.510
Average	0.560

HP

Serie Name	Ratio Value
autGVAex	0.811
aufF	0.491
autCDE	0.704
autGHI	0.581
autJK	0.525
eurGDPex	0.574
gerCDE	0.780
gerF	0.346
gerGHI	0.686
gerGVAex	0.894
gerJK	0.536
Average	0.630

BK

Serie Name	Ratio Value
autGVAex	0.833
aufF	0.547
autCDE	0.792
autGHI	0.629
autJK	0.338
eurGDPex	0.669
gerCDE	0.797
gerF	0.456
gerGHI	0.700
gerGVAex	0.898
gerJK	0.637
Average	0.663

Source: Own calculations.

Table A 7 a: Correlation between common parts of series and reference series

FOD

Serie Name	**(*)Lags**								
	-4	**-3**	**-2**	**-1**	**0**	**1**	**2**	**3**	**4**
autGVAex	-0.028	-0.079	0.029	-0.038	1	-0.038	0.029	-0.079	-0.028
aufF	-0.222	0.016	-0.158	-0.107	**0.821**	0.035	-0.175	0.077	-0.088
autCDE	0.12	-0.202	0.099	-0.044	**0.839**	0.1	0.173	-0.19	0.017
autGHI	-0.124	0.015	-0.067	0.105	**0.839**	0.205	0.12	-0.072	-0.065
autJK	0.001	0.134	0.228	0.033	**0.494**	-0.28	-0.126	-0.031	-0.095
eurGDPex	0.074	-0.091	0.092	0.214	**0.723**	0.092	-0.036	0.087	0.112
gerCDE	0.05	0.013	-0.012	0.18	**0.531**	0.129	0.14	0.061	-0.019
gerF	-0.086	-0.003	0.124	0.057	**0.557**	0.134	0.052	0.238	-0.08
gerGHI	-0.001	**0.202**	0.113	0.165	0.168	0.072	0.171	0.099	-0.041
gerGVAex	0.035	0.061	0.092	0.184	**0.426**	0.173	0.158	0.106	-0.048
gerJK	0.174	0.068	0.149	0.141	0.126	0.204	**0.304**	0.083	0.031

(*) High cross-correlations at positive lags indicates a leading behaviour of the variable with respect to the reference series.
Source: Own calculations.

Table A 7 b: Correlation between common parts of series and reference series

HP

Serie Name	**(*)Lags**								
	-4	**-3**	**-2**	**-1**	**0**	**1**	**2**	**3**	**4**
autGVAex	0.005	0.037	0.204	0.507	**1**	0.507	0.204	0.037	0.005
aufF	-0.033	-0.117	-0.092	0.13	**0.661**	0.221	-0.005	-0.031	0.006
autCDE	0.003	0.039	0.228	0.527	**0.965**	0.593	0.274	0.058	0.006
autGHI	-0.001	0.038	0.177	0.503	**0.962**	0.619	0.311	0.081	-0.008
autJK	0.056	0.08	0.108	0.102	**0.134**	-0.004	0.021	0.062	0.041
eurGDPex	0.011	0.075	0.271	0.564	**0.887**	0.574	0.312	0.14	0.005
gerCDE	0.013	0.099	0.276	0.548	**0.868**	0.581	0.313	0.106	-0.005
gerF	-0.071	0.007	0.202	0.45	**0.84**	0.508	0.235	0.078	-0.018
gerGHI	-0.011	0.183	0.399	0.594	**0.721**	0.471	0.278	0.107	0.004
gerGVAex	0.003	0.132	0.334	0.582	**0.845**	0.56	0.292	0.089	-0.011
gerJK	0.007	0.198	0.367	0.537	**0.671**	0.508	0.293	0.072	-0.034

(*) High cross-correlations at positive lags indicates a leading behaviour of the variable with respect to the reference series.

Source: Own calculations.

Table A 7 c: Correlation between common parts of series and reference series

BK

Serie Name	**(*)Lags**								
	-4	**-3**	**-2**	**-1**	**0**	**1**	**2**	**3**	**4**
autGVAex	-0.028	0.108	0.388	0.738	1	0.738	0.388	0.108	-0.028
aufF	-0.124	-0.097	0.079	0.365	**0.589**	0.425	0.164	-0.028	-0.08
autCDE	-0.025	0.112	0.378	0.706	**0.965**	0.743	0.431	0.162	0.011
autGHI	-0.031	0.067	0.299	0.619	**0.928**	0.778	0.517	0.264	0.086
autJK	0.016	0.061	0.099	0.075	-0.039	-0.124	-0.103	0.011	**0.13**
eurGDPex	0.018	0.141	0.363	0.634	**0.868**	0.711	0.478	0.258	0.105
gerCDE	0.045	0.181	0.408	0.676	**0.89**	0.706	0.449	0.214	0.06
gerF	-0.037	0.055	0.256	0.539	**0.836**	0.711	0.474	0.214	0.027
gerGHI	0.2	0.387	0.576	0.717	**0.778**	0.562	0.367	0.213	0.105
gerGVAex	0.119	0.276	0.494	0.728	**0.907**	0.698	0.437	0.201	0.044
gerJK	0.251	0.375	0.477	0.567	**0.661**	0.534	0.379	0.209	0.059

(*) High cross-correlations at positive lags indicates a leading behaviour of the variable with respect to the reference series.
Source: Own calculations.

Table A 8 a: Dynamic Factor Turning point analysis: leads and lags with respect to the reference series
Austrian gross value added excluding agriculture

FOD

	Peak	Trough	Peak	Trough	Peak	Trough	Peak	Trough	Peak	Trough	Peak	Trough	# of extra cycles
Reference Series	**Q4-1976**	**Q4-1977**	**Q4-1978**	**Q1-1980**	**Q4-1982**	**Q4-1986**	**Q3-1989**	**Q4-1992**	**Q4-1993**	**Q1-1995**	**Q1-1999**	**Q1-2001**	
aufF	-	0	0	5	0	9	7	-2	0	-	-	0	-1
autCDE	-	0	4	-	-	0	-4	-1	-	-	0	14	-3
autGHI	-	0	0	1	0	-2	0	-2	0	0	1	5	2
autJK	0	2	-	-	4	0	-4	3	3	-	3	2	0
eurGDPex	0	-	-	0	10	0	-4	0	0	1	2	1	0
gerCDE	-	-2	1	0	-6	10	-5	0	2	3	1	0	0
gerF	-	-3	-3	0	-7	-11	3	-3	0	-1	1	7	0
gerGHI	-	-2	1	0	-	-	-3	0	-	-	1	7	-3
gerGVAex	-	-3	1	0	-6	-	5	0	-	-	1	7	-2
gerJK	-	-	-2	2	-	-	5	-	-	-2	-1	7	-3

Note: *+(-) denotes a lag (lead) with respect to the reference series.*

Remark: Positive (negative) figures give the lagging (leading) quarters of the specific series compared to to the reference series turning point dates in the first line (in bold letters). A minus indicates a missing cycle.

Source: Own calculations.

Table A 8 b: Dynamic Factor Turning point analysis: leads and lags with respect to the reference series
Austrian gross value added excluding agriculture

HP

	Peak	Trough	Peak	Trough	Peak	Trough	Peak	Trough	Peak	Trough	# of extra cycles
Reference Series	**Q1-1980**	**Q4-1982**	**Q2-1986**	**Q1-1988**	**Q1-1992**	**Q1-1993**	**Q4-1994**	**Q1-1999**	**Q4-2000**	**Q4-2003**	
aufF	-9	0	4	-	-	0	-	9	-11	-	-1
autCDE	0	0	-	-	0	3	0	-8	0	-2	-1
autGHI	-2	0	-3	0	-2	0	0	0	0	0	1
autJK	-7	-12	-	-4	-6	3	3	1	1	-2	1
eurGDPex	0	0	-9	-	0	3	2	-8	-2	-2	0
gerCDE	0	0	0	0	-4	3	2	-8	1	-2	0
gerF	0	0	0	6	0	0	0	-	-3	-2	1
gerGHI	0	0	0	-2	-4	3	2	1	1	-2	2
gerGVAex	0	0	0	0	-4	3	2	-8	1	-2	0
gerJK	0	0	0	0	-4	8	6	-1	4	0	0

Note: *+(-) denotes a lag (lead) with respect to the reference series.*

Remark: Positive (negative) figures give the lagging (leading) quarters of the specific series compared to to the reference series turning point dates in the first line (in bold letters). A minus indicates a missing cycle.

Source: Own calculations.

Table A 8 c: Dynamic Factor Turning point analysis: leads and lags with respect to the reference series
Austrian gross value added excluding agriculture

BK

	Peak	Trough	Peak	Trough	Peak	Trough	Peak	Trough	Peak	Trough	Peak	Trough	# of extra cycles
Reference Series	**Q2-1977**	**Q2-1978**	**Q4-1979**	**Q4-1982**	**Q3-1985**	**Q4-1987**	**Q4-1991**	**Q3-1993**	**Q4-1994**	**Q1-1999**	**Q2-2000**	**Q2-2003**	
autF	0	1	0	-1	7	-	0	-3	0	-	-1	-8	1
autCDE	0	0	0	0	0	-1	1	0	1	0	1	0	1
autGHI	-1	-1	0	-1	1	1	0	-1	-2	-	-1	1	2
autJK	4	-5	-	2	-4	-2	-5	2	3	1	4	-1	0
eurGDPex	-1	0	0	0	-7	-1	-5	0	1	-8	1	0	1
gerCDE	-1	-1	0	0	0	0	-4	0	3	0	2	0	1
gerF	-1	0	1	-1	2	-2	1	-1	-1	-1	-1	-6	4
gerGHI	-	-	1	1	2	0	-4	1	3	0	2	1	0
gerGVAex	-1	-1	0	0	2	0	-3	0	4	0	2	1	1
gerJK	-1	-1	0	-4	4	3	-2	7	-	2	-8	2	1

Note: *+(-) denotes a lag (lead) with respect to the reference series.*

Remark: Positive (negative) figures give the lagging (leading) quarters of the specific series compared to to the reference series turning point dates in the first line (in bold letters). A minus indicates a missing cycle.

Source: Own calculations.

Table A 9 a: Dynamic Factor Analysis of turning point sequences with respect to the reference series Austrian gross value added excluding agriculture

FOD

	Average Lag at			Median Lag at		
w.r.t Reference Series	**P**	**T**	**All**	**P**	**T**	**All**
aufF	1.75	2.4	2.11	0	0	0
autCDE	0	3.25	1.86	-2	0	0
autGHI	0.2	0.33	0.27	0	0	0
autJK	1.2	1.75	1.44	1.5	2	2
eurGDPex	1.6	0.4	1	0	0	0
gerCDE	-1.4	1.83	0.36	-2	0	0
gerF	-1.2	-1.83	-1.55	-1.5	-2	-2
gerGHI	-0.33	1.25	0.57	-1	0	0
gerGVAex	0.25	1	0.63	1	0	0.5
gerJK	0.67	2.33	1.5	-1.5	0	0.5

Note: *+(-) denotes a lag (lead) with respect to the reference series.*

Source: Own calcualtions.

Table A 9 b: Dynamic Factor Analysis of turning point sequences with respect to the reference series Austrian gross value added excluding agriculture

HP

	Average Lag at			Median Lag at		
w.r.t Reference Series	**P**	**T**	**All**	**P**	**T**	**All**
aufF	-5.33	3	-1.17	-10	0	0
autCDE	0	-1.75	-0.88	0	-1	0
autGHI	-1.4	0	-0.7	-2	0	0
autJK	-2.25	-2.8	-2.56	-2.5	-3	-3
eurGDPex	-1.8	-1.75	-1.78	-1	-1	-1
gerCDE	-0.2	-1.4	-0.8	0	-1	0
gerF	-0.6	1	0.11	0	0	0
gerGHI	-0.2	0	-0.1	0	-1	0
gerGVAex	-0.2	-1.4	-0.8	0	-1	0
gerJK	1.2	1.4	1.3	0	0	0

Note: *+(-) denotes a lag (lead) with respect to the reference series.*

Source: Own calcualtions.

Table A 9 c: Dynamic Factor Analysis of turning point sequences with respect to the reference series Austrian gross value added excluding agriculture

BK

	Average Lag at			Median Lag at		
w.r.t Reference Series	**P**	**T**	**All**	**P**	**T**	**All**
aufF	1	-2.75	-0.5	0	-2	0
autCDE	0.5	-0.17	0.17	0.5	0	0
autGHI	-0.5	-0.2	-0.36	-0.5	-1	-1
autJK	0.4	-0.5	-0.09	-0.5	0	0
eurGDPex	-1.83	-1.5	-1.67	-0.5	0	0
gerCDE	0	-0.17	-0.08	0	0	0
gerF	0.17	-1.83	-0.83	0	-1	-1
gerGHI	0.8	0.6	0.7	1.5	0.5	1
gerGVAex	0.67	0	0.33	1	0	0
gerJK	-1.4	1.5	0.18	-1.5	2	-0.5

***N ote:** +(-) denotes a lag (lead) with respect to the reference series.*

Source: Own calcualtions.

Table A 10 a: Dynamic Factor Analysis of cycles with respect to the reference series Austrian gross value added excluding agriculture

FOD

Phases and cycles average duration</TH< TR>				
	P to T	**P to P**	**T to P**	**T to T**
Reference Series	**8.5**	**17**	**9.2**	**17.8**
aufF	17	24.75	7.6	22.5
autCDE	22	38	13.67	35
autGHI	7.29	13.57	6.75	13.14
autJK	9.67	17.6	8.2	17.8
eurGDPex	8.83	17.4	9	16.2
gerCDE	5.5	15.4	10.33	15
gerF	8.17	16.2	9	16.33
gerGHI	11.33	40	22.67	33.33
gerGVAex	7.5	26.33	18.25	25
gerJK	13.33	40.5	29	44

Source: Own calculations.

Table A 10 b: Dynamic Factor Analysis of cycles with respect to the reference series Austrian gross value added excluding agriculture

HP

Phases and cycles average duration</TH< TR>				
	P to T	**P to P**	**T to P**	**T to T**
Reference Series	**10.2**	**20**	**11**	**20.25**
aufF	18.67	35.33	17.33	36.5
autCDE	9.25	27	18.67	26.67
autGHI	8.33	16.2	9.4	16
autJK	9.5	17.4	8.6	18
eurGDPex	8.2	19.5	13	19.75
gerCDE	9	20.25	12	19.75
gerF	8.33	17.6	11	19.4
gerGHI	7.43	13.17	6.83	12.83
gerGVAex	9	20.25	12	19.75
gerJK	10.4	21	10.75	20.25

Source: Own calculations.

Table A 10 c: Dynamic Factor Analysis of cycles with respect to the reference series Austrian gross value added excluding agriculture

BK

Phases and cycles average duration</TH< TR>				
	P to T	**P to P**	**T to P**	**T to T**
Reference Series	**10.17**	**17.6**	**8.6**	**19.2**
aufF	6.71	14.33	8.17	14.33
autCDE	7.57	14.67	8.5	15.83
autGHI	7.57	14.86	8.14	16.17
autJK	9.67	17.6	7.67	16.5
eurGDPex	10.5	17.5	7.83	19.2
gerCDE	8	15	8.17	16
gerF	5.89	11.22	6.22	10.88
gerGHI	8.67	15.8	8.4	15.6
gerGVAex	7.57	15	8.83	16.17
gerJK	7.29	16	9.33	16.33

Source: Own calculations.

Forschungsergebnisse der Wirtschaftsuniversität Wien

Herausgeber: Wirtschaftsuniversität Wien –
vertreten durch a.o. Univ. Prof. Dr. Barbara Sporn

Band	1	Stefan Felder: Frequenzallokation in der Telekommunikation. Ökonomische Analyse der Vergabe von Frequenzen unter besonderer Berücksichtigung der UMTS-Auktionen. 2004.
Band	2	Thomas Haller: Marketing im liberalisierten Strommarkt. Kommunikation und Produktplanung im Privatkundenmarkt. 2005.
Band	3	Alexander Stremitzer: Agency Theory: Methodology, Analysis. A Structured Approach to Writing Contracts. 2005.
Band	4	Günther Sedlacek: Analyse der Studiendauer und des Studienabbruch-Risikos. Unter Verwendung der statistischen Methoden der Ereignisanalyse. 2004.
Band	5	Monika Knassmüller: Unternehmensleitbilder im Vergleich. Sinn- und Bedeutungsrahmen deutschsprachiger Unternehmensleitbilder – Versuch einer empirischen (Re-)Konstruktion. 2005.
Band	6	Matthias Fink: Erfolgsfaktor Selbstverpflichtung bei vertrauensbasierten Kooperationen. Mit einem empirischen Befund. 2005.
Band	7	Michael Gerhard Kraft: Ökonomie zwischen Wissenschaft und Ethik. Eine dogmenhistorische Untersuchung von Léon M.E. Walras bis Milton Friedman. 2005.
Band	8	Ingrid Zechmeister: Mental Health Care Financing in the Process of Change. Challenges and Approaches for Austria. 2005.
Band	9	Sarah Meisenberger: Strukturierte Organisationen und Wissen. 2005.
Band	10	Anne-Katrin Neyer: Multinational teams in the European Commission and the European Parliament. 2005.
Band	11	Birgit Trukeschitz: Im Dienst Sozialer Dienste. Ökonomische Analyse der Beschäftigung in sozialen Dienstleistungseinrichtungen des Nonprofit Sektors. 2006
Band	12	Marcus Kölling: Interkulturelles Wissensmanagement. Deutschland Ost und West. 2006.
Band	13	Ulrich Berger: The Economics of Two-way Interconnection. 2006.
Band	14	Susanne Guth: Interoperability of DRM Systems. Exchanging and Processing XML-based Rights Expressions. 2006.
Band	15	Bernhard Klement: Ökonomische Kriterien und Anreizmechanismen für eine effiziente Förderung von industrieller Forschung und Innovation. Mit einer empirischen Quantifizierung der Hebeleffekte von F&E-Förderinstrumenten in Österreich. 2006.
Band	16	Markus Imgrund: Wege aus der Insolvenz. Eine Analyse der Fortführung und Sanierung insolventer Klein- und Mittelbetriebe unter besonderer Berücksichtigung des Konfigurationsansatzes. 2007.
Band	17	Nicolas Knotzer: Product Recommendations in E-Commerce Retailing Applications. 2008.
Band	18	Astrid Dickinger: Perceived Quality of Mobile Services. A Segment-Specific Analysis. 2007.
Band	19	Nadine Wiedermann-Ondrej: Hybride Finanzierungsinstrumente in der nationalen und internationalen Besteuerung der USA. 2008.
Band	20	Helmut Sorger: Entscheidungsorientiertes Risikomanagement in der Industrieunternehmung. 2008.
Band	21	Martin Rietsch: Messung und Analyse des ökonomischen Wechselkursrisikos aus Unternehmenssicht: Ein stochastischer Simulationsansatz. 2008.

Band 22 Hans Christian Mantler: Makroökonomische Effizienz des Finanzsektors. Herleitung eines theoretischen Modells und Schätzung der Wachstumsimplikationen für die Marktwirtschaften und Transformationsökonomien Europas. 2008.

Band 23 Youri Tacoun: La théorie de la valeur de Christian von Ehrenfels. 2008.

Band 24 Monika Koller: Longitudinale Betrachtung der Kognitiven Dissonanz. Eine Tagebuchstudie zur Reiseentscheidung. 2008.

Band 25 Marcus Scheiblecker: The Austrian Business Cycle in the European Context. 2008.

Band 26 Aida Numic: Multinational Teams in European and American Companies. 2008.

Band 27 Ulrike Bauernfeind: User Satisfaction with Personalised Internet Applications. 2008.

www.peterlang.de

Peter Lang · Internationaler Verlag der Wissenschaften

Steffen Kern

The Behaviour of Interest Groups in Trade and Industry Towards Monetary Policy and Central Banks

Theory and Evidence on Germany and the Euro Area

Frankfurt am Main, Berlin, Bern, Bruxelles, New York, Oxford, Wien, 2006.
381 pp., num. fig., tab. and graf.
Studien zu Internationalen Wirtschaftsbeziehungen. Edited by Michael Frenkel.
Vol. 6
ISBN 978-3-631-54615-4 · pb. € 59.70*

This study investigates the behaviour of private interest groups towards monetary policy and central banks. It explores the extent to which interest groups seek to influence monetary policy and their motivations for doing so – or for refraining from doing so. Where evidence for interest group activity with respect to monetary decisions can be found, the study aims to identify the ways in which groups communicate with policymakers. The behaviour of interest groups in the area of monetary policymaking is investigated by means of an empirical case study of the relations between interest groups and the Deutsche Bundesbank in Germany as well as the potential impact of introduction of the single European currency and establishment of the ECB. The study evaluates the relevance of the institutional setting, policy issues and other factors.

Contents: Monetary policymaking in Germany · Institutional context: the Deutsche Bundesbank · Issue context: monetary policy in Germany · Exposure of trade and industry to monetary policy · Group context: industry and trade associations in Germany · Analysis of interest group behaviour in Germany and at EU level · Interest group activity after entry into EMU · Channels of communication of interests

Frankfurt am Main · Berlin · Bern · Bruxelles · New York · Oxford · Wien
Distribution: Verlag Peter Lang AG
Moosstr. 1, CH-2542 Pieterlen
Telefax 0041 (0) 32/376 17 27

*The €-price includes German tax rate
Prices are subject to change without notice

Homepage http://www.peterlang.de